65

ASSISTED BY: Campbell Campbell, Aisha Catena, Annie Dills, Sophia Durose, Lizzy Lemieux, Davis Mendez, Conor O'Brien, Paz O'Farrell, Finn O'Neil, Emma Theiss, Selena Trager, Alvaro Villanueva, Isabella Zou. COPY EDITOR: Caitlin Van Dusen. SALES AND DISTRIBUTION MANAGER: Dan Weiss. PUBLISHING ASSOCIATE: Eric Cromie. TECHNOLOGY DIRECTOR: Brian Christian. ART DIRECTOR: Sunra Thompson. FOUNDING EDITOR: Dave Eggers. EXECUTIVE DIRECTOR: Amanda Uhle. EDITOR: Claire Boyle.

GUEST EDITORS: Valeria Luiselli, with Heather Cleary

COVER AND INTERIOR ILLUSTRATIONS: Rachel Levit Ruiz.

MCSWEENEY'S PUBLISHING BOARD: Natasha Boas, Kyle Bruck, Carol Davis, Brian Dice (president), Isabel Duffy-Pinner, Dave Eggers, Caterina Fake, Hilary Kivitz, Jordan Kurland, Nion McEvoy, Gina Pell, Jeremy Radcliffe, Jed Repko, Julia Slavin, Vendela Vida.

Printed in Canada.

With translations by Heather Cleary, Gabriela Jauregui,
Megan McDowell, Julia Sanches, Jennifer Shyue, and Jenna Tang.

DEAR MCSWEENEY'S,

I traveled to the Yucatán Peninsula in early 2020. I wanted to be re-introduced to a city on the banks of the Grijalva River where I'd lived between the ages of two and six. It's not a city I chose, and I wasn't born there. My parents and I moved there in 1984 because my father had been offered a job. That tropical city, all jungle and water, was the place of my emotional and sensorial birth. I went back twice at most when I was a teenager, so when I got off the bus in January, I was surprised to discover the power its scent had over me. It was the smell of my childhood. The most animal part of my brain recognized it immediately—thick with humidity, but also: mud, tulips smelling wild, baskets woven from palm fronds, caramelized papaya sweets, nance fruits rotting on the sidewalks by the thousand. Because that city was, if nothing else, a vast cyclorama of flora and fauna. Caimans in its swampland ponds, red ants, possums, palms, iguanas, water hyacinths, trees with yellow flowers and trees with pink flowers. I began to miss this jungle procession as soon as we returned to Mexico City.

After leaving that riverside city, I extended my trip through archaeological ruins and cities I'd never known, places where I felt both enchanted and connected by a thin genealogical root—thin but deeply embedded. My paternal grandfather was born in a small town called Progreso on the Yucatán Peninsula; it now has a modern shipping terminal on a jetty that stretches several kilometers into the sea, along which cargo trucks drive back and forth. My paternal grandmother was born on Isla Mujeres in Quintana Roo; among other economic activities, she hunted sea turtles as a child. Her nose still bears the diagonal trace of a gash from a flipper. I didn't go to Chetumal much when I was younger—because it was far away, and also because of the complicated emotions my father felt when he was there. It's the city where he was born, but it's also the corner of the world he fled. His original birth certificate says he was born in the territory of Quintana Roo rather than a state in the Mexican republic, because in the late 1950s, Quintana Roo wasn't yet an independent state. At the end of the nineteenth century, the area was a penal colony, an open prison that didn't need walls or barricades aside from the jungle of mahogany, howler monkeys, and jaguars on one side and the Caribbean on the other. My father grew up in a paradise where, at the same time, the most intellectual profession he could aspire to was becoming a schoolteacher. He left when he was fourteen and never moved back. His memories of the place are both dazzling for their natural beauty and raw for the conditions of poverty in which he lived. For reasons unknown to any of us, he suffers from a depression that he manages well enough with prescriptions; his two children (my brother and I) inherited this trait and also turn to chemistry to relieve the symptoms of a sickness known, in other centuries, as melancholia. Lately, I've taken to calling it my open prison.

Almost nothing remains of the vast jungle that once served as a prison wall. It was devoured by the sawmills that brought a kind of economic well-being to a tropical zone of incandescent, and occasionally melancholic, beauty.

The largest tree on the Yucatán Peninsula isn't the ceiba but the guanacaste, with its umbrellalike crown (its branches are much longer than its trunk is tall), delicate leaves, and white flowers like tufts of cotton. Its wood isn't as hard or as beautiful as mahogany, which has saved it from extinction, and its seedpods look a bit like the swirls of Mayan glyphs. On my trip, I found one on the side of the highway and thought it couldn't have been a coincidence. I'm not sure, but I suspect that those distant, legendary relatives of ours gathered their glyphs into an alphabet of flora that has somehow survived in this birthplace of green.

Signing off,

CLAUDINA DOMINGO
MEXICO CITY, MEXICO
(TRANSLATED BY HEATHER CLEARY)

DEAR MCSWEENEY'S,
I don't remember the first time I saw an illustration of a beautiful, exalted brown woman surrounded by flora on some Latinx empowerment website, but they're all over the place. I always find them when I'm doomscrolling. It occurs to me that you might have seen what I'm talking about, some likeness of me naked and crouching but producing. The smartest people in my community know that these bodies, bodies like mine, are sexualized and dehumanized by members of the political right. But the radical deflection from that—this image of the wise, giving, patient brown woman with an inherent connection to the land that internet Latinxism counters the mainstream propaganda with is inescapably maternalist. *Good girls become mothers*, it says. *But bad girls are fertile too*. There's a popular inspirational quote that goes around Latinx Instagram: "When you buried us, you didn't know you made us stronger, because you didn't know we were seeds." To resist means to bear life.

When we are writers, we birth books. When we have worked for a lifetime on a passion project, we say, "This is my baby." I've been asked what the labor was like for my first book. I've puffed out my stomach under a billowy dress, put my hand on my belly, and smiled softly into a mirror, already seeing myself as prettier, more gentle, like Meghan Markle in her maternity portraits, who looked like the most glorious human alive.

But I have worked my whole life to be able to be childless, and I relish it. It is an extremely personal decision, but it casts some votes in public. Since both the right and left have a stake in the image of beautiful and bountiful brown bodies, my willful barrenness—bearing nothing young, simply discarding pretty old thoughts, picturesque carcasses of my old selves—dispels at least one myth. The myth that, like our planet, Latina women will always be around, long-suffering and giving, withstanding any pain, with no beginning and no end, ever patient, the foundation of everything their children are, no matter how much we drill into them. So we exist. We are beautiful to look at, to think about, to touch about, under the aura of muchness and eternal spring, as the ocean catches fire and the Earth dies.

Goodbye,

KARLA CORNEJO VILLAVICENCIO
NEW HAVEN, CT

DEAR MCSWEENEY'S,

An insect lives in the corners of my house. Mom says we have to kill it and clean the house over and over until all the others like it go away. Mom hates it, and I hate that I'm supposed to kill a creature I don't know. Why should I be afraid of it? How is this fear born? Could I maybe grow more and more different, grow closer to what seems strange? When you turn out the lights, the sun is rising on other worlds. An orchestra of tiny, fragile bodies comes to inhabit every corner of the earth, and yet we choose to sleep.

Later, I heard someone call this insect "una cucaracha." *Una* means it's feminine. A she. She is large, mysterious, and utterly insectile—quiet and red like a sunset, she presents a pair of dangerous desires to those who choose to see her from a different angle. The cockroach inhabits my dreams and becomes my mirror: she appears and is multiplied.

I really want to meet this bug they're always talking about, but Mom says I can't. Every night when she falls asleep I want to try, but our time will come. When I see a cockroach, I imagine what might happen if my fingertips were to brush against her. Would something of her maybe transfer to me? It feels as if my skin were calling out for the shine of her exoskeleton—as if, little by little, I were beginning to transform. My fantasies course through me and I feel spines poking through my legs and I feel my pupils growing big and black until they cover the entire surface of my eyes. My voice becomes a hiss and my body falls away. Slowly it falls and soon my skin isn't; my body is wrapped with a new one.

When are you a cockroach? When are you an exterminator?

You might not be able to see with your eyes what's hiding in the dark of night, but if you open your ears and let the sound in through your nostrils, other ways of seeing will reveal themselves to you. Let's let the minuscule inhabit us, again and again. Let's let dreams, eclipsed between our lips, tell the stories that through fear become deep, symbolic desires. Subtle wonders.

Their antennae, the most fragile part of their bodies. Six spine-covered legs that stand in every corner. A shell concealing two wings ready to spread at the hint of human presence—to frighten only: flight is no longer an option. Her stealthy movements heavy with meaning, she appears and hides again; no can find her or chase her; people desire her extermination, but I am seduced by her cunning, her mystery, and all the desires she awakens in me. There is so much of her in me, and so little of me in her.

When I talk about cockroaches, people often get a strange look on their faces—they can't believe anyone could feel tenderness, love, or admiration for a cockroach. But cockroaches are like mirrors; I see myself in them: vulnerable, resilient, and in an endless state of transformation. The body, when it announces its strange wonders and its infinite metamorphoses, is in fact announcing that this, this is no matter for the faint of heart.

How many times has a cockroach looked for itself on the floor on a starry night?

A dream:

There was a girl in my dreams who spoke in secret with the cockroaches that had infested her room after their fumigated defeat in a kitchen they had once called home. One Thursday afternoon that girl felt a movement in her body. The whole city had begun to quake. A shrill voice called to her. "Come here," trilled the cockroach, whose head was poking out from a crack in the wall, and the girl, her own voice trembling with fear, replied:

"It's all falling apart."

And the cockroach answered with her camouflaged voice, with her wise, spiny voice: "Or maybe it's all falling into place."

The cockroach grew and grew and together they watched the city crumble.

No story that involves cockroaches will have a happy ending.

An un-conclusion:

Where does all this repulsion come from? How can we love the strangeness and wonder of what seems like the final frontier of affect? Which bodies embody the cockroach? Why is it so important to think about her when we think about the world? These are some of the questions I ask myself whenever I'm around these feared but resilient beings. Persistent, they devour tidiness like we do; we others, we strange ones, we trans* women.

The cockroach. She, we. We other transmuting shes.

How can we see ourselves in her?

Thank you for reading and feeling me through a thing that sparks fear. I am very much a cockroach, it's why I write.

LIA GARCÍA (LA NOVIA SIRENA)
MEXICO CITY, ON A CLOUDY DAY
(TRANSLATED BY HEATHER CLEARY)

DEAR MCSWEENEY'S,

In the summer of 2009, I set out on a three-month trek. My purpose in hiking the Ayuujk Trail, as I called it, was to visit the communities in the Mixe region, northeast of Oaxaca's capital, and to see the old routes that had remained in use even after highways established new ones. During that period of intense learning, I tried to avoid walking alone in the woods after dark, but I relaxed my precautions as the days went by until one night I found myself in a pine-and-oak forest in the middle of a fierce summer storm. Stories passed down from one generation to the next had taught me that pine trees are perfect lightning rods. My great-great-aunt Guadalupe's husband once fell asleep at the base of a pine tree. He'd been drinking pulque at a local stand and decided to rest for a minute on his way back to the ranch. His friends left him there, right where they later found his body among the charred splinters of a pine that had been split in half by lightning. My family has many stories about the power of lightning, stories I could tell now to make absolutely clear how terrified I was to find myself in that situation. The lightning illuminated the forest and my fear-soaked face; the thunder sent waves through the Earth's crust that, together with the heavy rain, knocked me off-balance. In the throes of that desperate situation, I understood, as I never had before, the reasons we worship nature. I remembered the words the elders used when asking nature to temper its hostility, the phrases they used when they had to labor in unfamiliar forests and needed nature to hold back its most dangerous animals: "Hold fast the animals of your creation, those that could bite us, those that could kill us, hold fast your creatures, let us be, for we, too, are your creation." You could say that the essence of the Ayuujk cosmovision is seeing the land as a living thing we are part of; we are at the mercy of its cycles, and it has the power to make us disappear with one shudder of its pelt.

These ideas contrast sharply with the way certain kinds of environmental activism talk about the natural world. We all agree on the prognosis: Capitalism is driving our planet to a point of no return that puts our very existence in danger. In this context, every struggle and social movement defines itself differently, because the climate crisis disrupts—and will continue to disrupt—everything. The people who have contributed least to this crisis will suffer its effects far more profoundly than those who have benefitted from destroying the planet. This crisis stems in part from an idea that underlies the discourse of development and capitalist progress: that human beings are categorically separate from nature. According to this idea, the natural world is a source of raw materials, of natural resources transformed into commodities. Several responses to the climate crisis have emerged from the Western tradition and have been categorized as environmental activism. This label, however, contains vastly divergent and even opposing positions, so we should approach it with caution.

Even the best versions of Western environmental activism—not the kinds that flirt with eco-fascism or the ones that propose technological solutions solely to perpetuate the capitalist mode of production—are framed in this way. Though those environmental movements may be genuinely concerned about climate crisis, the idea central to them that nature is a living, now feeble, thing that must be rescued and cared for by human beings still adheres to the Western conception of humans as separate from nature: human beings—at a remove from the natural world—must protect nature, which they had been treating as a source of raw materials. Though the intention behind this separation is the opposite of what it used to be, the separation remains. Now we must care for the very thing we once exploited: that antipode of culture, of humanity; the Other that is the Western idea of nature.

Perhaps this is why Western environmental activism has had trouble integrating itself with other movements fighting the destruction of the planet. Rather than viewing nature as an Other to care for, many non-Western traditions hold that human beings *are* nature, that people are but one more type of animal in the ecosystem. The lands of Indigenous peoples have been and continue to be exploited, turned into commodities, and plundered for raw materials in development projects; this plundering is inextricably linked to climate crisis. The resistance to this plundering— which has gone on uninterrupted for the last five hundred years—is now, in the capitalist present, also a fight against climate crisis. The defense of the land by non-Western peoples, the fight against mining companies and extractivist megaprojects, is inscribed within the logic that we are part of nature. This is why, instead of "environmental activism," we say "defense of the land." To confront this crisis, we need to bring environmental activists and land defenders together. And we're running out of time.

Amuum tu'uk joojt,

YÁSNAYA ELENA AGUILAR GIL
AYUTLA MIXE, OAXACA
(TRANSLATED BY HEATHER CLEARY)

A version of this text appeared in El país *under the title "Jëtsuk. Nuestro ambientalismo se llama defensa del territorio."*

INTRODUCTION

by VALERIA LUISELLI
and HEATHER CLEARY

AMERICA HAS ENDURED FIVE hundred years of plundering. Exactly five hundred years ago, after almost two years of relentless warfare, the largest city in America fell to European dominion. The great Tenochtitlán—now the historic center of Mexico City—was seized in 1521 by Hernán Cortés and his men, who had disembarked on Mexican shores following a rumor, spread by Christopher Columbus almost three decades earlier, of abundant stores of gold in the "new" continent. Before the Spaniards attacked Tenochtitlán, the Mexica emperor Moctezuma had given Cortés a map drawn on a piece of nequen, detailing all the rivers running north of the city where gold dust was regularly collected. Once he was sure there was gold in the region, Cortés proceeded to invade Tenochtitlán, imprison Moctezuma, and sack the Mexica treasury.

Similarly, in 1532, Francisco Pizarro and his men ambushed and held for ransom the Inca ruler Atahualpa, who controlled modern-day Peru, Bolivia, Ecuador, and parts of Chile, Colombia, and Argentina. To buy his freedom, Atahualpa filled one large room with golden artifacts and two with silver. Metals had been crafted in the region for at least three thousand years prior to the arrival of the Europeans, so by the time Pizarro arrived, the Incas were making highly complex artwork with gold, such as miniature gardens that simulated earth with gold granules, gold figures of men, llamas, and corn stalks. Oblivious to their craftsmanship, Pizarro's men melted the artifacts that Atahualpa surrendered, cast them into neat rectangular bars, and sent them back to Spain. Atahualpa, in return, was not granted his freedom. He was tortured, forcibly converted to Catholicism, baptized "Francisco" after the conqueror, and publicly strangled.

The stories continue. There is Francisco Vásquez de Coronado, who in 1540 led an expedition to modern-day Arizona, New Mexico, Oklahoma, and Kansas, feverishly looking for the (non-existent) "Seven Cities of Gold." There is Nuño de Guzmán and his nephew Diego de Guzmán, voracious slave raiders, who instituted a system of slave trade across Mexico in the 1520s. Nuño de Guzmán later tortured the Tarascan leader Tangaxuan II to get him to reveal the supposed secret locations of stores of gold in what is now Michoacán. There was no gold, and Tangaxuan II was dragged by a horse through the streets and burned alive in 1530. He also was baptized "Francisco" before being killed

Always gold, always what they wanted back in Spain was gold. And if not gold, then silver. Between 1500 and 1650, the Spaniards extracted 181 tons of gold and 16,000 tons of silver from America. In return, they brought a mixed bag: smallpox, horses, the Spanish language, Catholicism, Cervantes, guns. They brought a new economy too: one based on mining, indentured servitude, and slavery on a scale never before seen on the continent. Between 1525 and the late 1800s, more than 5 million Indigenous Americans and more than 12.5 million Africans were enslaved—in mines and, later, in agriculture.

When it was no longer silver or gold, it was sugar. Columbus had brought sugar to the Caribbean, to what is today Haiti and the Dominican Republic, and the plant, a grass, grew quick and bountifully. Sugar—or "white gold," as it was called—was highly coveted in Europe, and the increasing demand led to a rapid mass systematization of indentured servitude and to the consolidation of slavery across the continent. This system expanded in successive waves as new crops joined the market, and schooners, galleys, and naval ships triangled across the Atlantic—between Africa and America, and from America to Europe. After sugar came tobacco, coffee, cacao, and cotton. As Eduardo Galeano writes in *Open Veins of Latin America: Five Centuries of the Pillage of a Continent*, a book that is fifty years old yet still entirely current: "The more coveted by the global market, the larger the misfortune that a product brings to the Latin American people who, with their sacrifice, have to produce it." Indeed, now that avocados have become the "green gold" Mexico exports to the United States, generating nearly three billion dollars in revenue per year, farmers in the state of Michoacán are being murdered, extorted, or displaced by drug cartels, often in concert with government officials and international captains of industry, secure in their impunity.

Across America, from the northern prairies to the southern pampas, land was grabbed, claimed, and partitioned into brutal ways of producing: latifundios, ingenios, haciendas, plantations. And later partitioned, also, into ruthless ways of belonging and excluding: settlements, reservations, and later, in the cities, favelas, solares, tugurios, projects. During the colonial period in America, the particular ways in which European powers usurped land, settled it (such a dainty word for such a violent act), and managed it differed in detail but not in essence. The Portuguese, Dutch, French,

British, and Spanish all enslaved and exploited in order to extract whatever the land yielded.

As European power began to wane and the former colonies gained independence, a new power took hold, reproducing many of the old mechanisms and systems. As early as 1891, in his seminal essay "Our América," José Martí heralded the arrival of the United States as the new colonizing force that would take the seat left empty by the European powers. Referring to "our América," or the Latin portion of the continent, he writes: "The hour is near when she will be approached by an enterprising and forceful nation that will demand intimate relations with her, though it does not know her and disdains her." And, of course, he was right. In 1898, the United States took over Cuba; the following year it took over Puerto Rico and still has not let go; 1899 also marked the founding of the United Fruit Company, the still-existing corporation (now Chiquita) through which the category of the "banana republic" came into being. (To the Latin American ear, the liberality with which the term *banana republic* is still dispensed by news anchors, politicians, and journalists in the United States is, to say the least, ironic: they seem to disdain the mess they themselves created.)

The United Fruit Company monopolized not only the fruit trade in Central America but also the management of basic services in the region: the electricity, post office, telegraph, telephone, railroads, and maritime routes. It took control, as well, of the political administration of the countries themselves, meddling in all domestic affairs. Neruda writes in *Canto General* (as translated by Jack Schmitt): "When the trumpet sounded / everything was prepared on earth, / and Jehovah gave the world / to Coca-Cola Inc., Anaconda, / Ford Motors, and other corporations. / The United Fruit Company / reserved for itself the most juicy piece, / the central coast of my world." Meanwhile, the plundering continued north of the Rio Bravo as well: treaties regarding Indigenous lands were routinely ignored; residential schools stole children from their families as part of a "civilizing" project. And then there was the concatenation of horrors known as the Jim Crow laws (and their less codified afterlives).

The US stronghold in Central America continued through the twentieth century, with administrations successively funding military dictatorships and civil wars. There was, for example, the 1954 coup d'état against Jacobo Árbenz in Guatemala—backed by the CIA at the urging of the United Fruit Company—which destabilized democracy in the country and led to thirty-six years of civil war and genocide that took more than two hundred thousand lives, predominantly of Mayan peoples. In this same period, from 1979 to 1992, the Carter and Reagan administrations funded a long and ruthless civil war in El Salvador, during which the military-led government relentlessly massacred left-wing opposition groups and civilians alike. Around one-fifth of the population of El Salvador had to flee the country. The aftershocks of these interventions come, still today, in waves of displaced adults and children who now seek asylum in the United States, and upon arrival are locked up in camps, shelters, detention centers, and cages.

US interventions did not stop at the Panama Canal but extended into the Southern Cone. One of the most well-known instances is the US-backed Chilean coup d'état against Salvador

Allende, who had nationalized US-owned copper mines in Chile. Aided by the CIA, on September 11, 1973, Chilean troops seized the seat of government, Allende took his own life as the soldiers stormed his office, and Augusto Pinochet began a vicious dictatorship that would loom over Chile for the next seventeen years. The coup was part of a broader series of military interventions in the region known as Operation Condor, which, under cover of Cold War scare tactics, sought to eliminate those leaders who were not inclined to offer favorable terms for US trade with their nations, or who, heaven forbid, resisted the privatization of their natural resources.

This issue features works that explore these forms of past and present colonial violence and that look at the effects of this violence on both the land and bodies across America. At the same time, they reveal diverse forms of resistance. They dig below the surface of deserts and decadent nightclubs, explore the questionable cultural politics of museums and theme parks, and take us into prisons of both body and mind. After Karen Tei Yamashita and Ronaldo Lopes de Oliveira's bracing reboot of the Brazilian modernist Oswald de Andrade's 1928 "Cannibalist Manifesto" (which gleefully gnawed on the bones of the European canon), we're transported to the Musée du Quai Branly, where we find Gabriela Wiener (translated by Gabriela Jauregui) examining her reflection in a glass case that houses the cultural patrimony stolen from her native Peru by her own great-grandfather. The institutional space of the museum is also central to Laia Jufresa's short story "Colorscape," which drops the reader into the middle of a performance art piece about state violence and forced disappearance in Latin America. Carlos Manuel

Álvarez (translated by Julia Sanches) writes a firsthand account of a recent hunger strike in Cuba, addressing the government's marginalization and persecution of Black and Brown bodies, while Sophie Braxton, in "Flat Earth Society," explores the psychology of alienation as it relates to both labor and human connections in the southern United States.

Shifting gears, we get a dizzying dog's-eye view of the historical layers of Mexico City/Tenochtitlán in Gabriela Jauregui's "The Island," and then follow the Pan-American Highway through the bone-riddled sands of the Peruvian desert in Julia Wong Kcomt's "Chimbote Highway" (translated by Jennifer Shyue), before watching the Mexican countryside quake and split open in Brenda Lozano's "A Volcano Is Born" (translated by Heather Cleary). In each of these texts—as in Mahogany L. Browne's incandescent "Reft of a Nation," the poem at both the sequential and the ethical center of the collection—the fires of the earth and the injustices it has witnessed refuse to be contained.

Next, Samanta Schweblin's "An Unlucky Man" (translated by Megan McDowell) and Sabrina Helen Li's "Worldly Wonders" explore different forms of strength under conditions of vulnerability; in the first, a little girl navigates both a family crisis and an intimate crisis of her own; in the second, a young woman's body is exoticized and infantilized for public consumption at a nationality-themed amusement park. The next pair of stories introduces us to two men displaced by very different circumstances, trying to rebuild their lives: the narrator of Edmundo Paz Soldán's "El Señor de La Palma" (translated by Jenna Tang) finds himself embroiled in a cult (or is it just a pyramid scheme?) as he flees the dubious legalities of his own past, while the protagonist of Nimmi Gowrinathan's "One Man and His Island" is a refugee trying to cultivate Sri Lanka in a tiny corner of Los Angeles.

And then there are the bodies bound: MJ Bond draws a bright, pain-streaked line between the body in transition and the molecular structures of glass and obsidian; in "Ain't Them Bodies Saints," C. T. Mexica takes us inside prison walls that cannot keep the mind from soaring, while a letter from Claudina Domingo reminds us that the mind itself can also be a prison. Also in the issue's letters, Yásnaya Elena Aguilar Gil reminds us of the importance of recognizing non-Western conceptions of the natural world and our relationship with it; Karla Cornejo Villavicencio asserts her right not to reproduce; and Lia García (La Novia Sirena) shares a lyrical reflection on bodies labeled and persecuted as monstrous, and why we should consider the cockroach.

The pieces selected for this issue draw on diverse traditions and aesthetics, and more than half are translations. By placing these authors from different latitudes within the same pages, it becomes obvious that neatly defining American identities is an impossible and absurd task. As Natalie Díaz said in an interview for *The Rumpus* in 2020, identity is often weaponized, particularly in the United States, "as a thing to pin us down and hold us still... I am imagining ways to become unpinnable." The unpinnable cannot be extracted; it cannot be plundered, swallowed, homogenized, commodified.

Among the many questions we discussed as we worked with these texts, one kept coming up: What to do with the accent in *América*? Such an apparently trivial thing—a small typographical mark—but one that carries so much political weight. Should we keep the diacritic as it appears in Spanish, offering a visual reminder to the reader that America is not a country but a continent[1]? Or should we "translate" *América* by removing the accent, and in doing so challenge the Anglophone reader in the United States to pause and look at this familiar word anew?

We went back and forth with the translators. We went back and forth among ourselves. We turned once again to Martí's "Our América" and to its translator, Esther Allen. When we asked her to share the thought process behind her choice to keep the diacritic, she responded:

> In the Penguin Classics anthology I did of Martí's selected writings, there's a version of "Our America" without the accent mark; at that point I didn't think one was needed. The essay itself makes it pretty damn clear what he's talking about, even specifying the region's geographic boundaries in the final paragraph: "del Bravo a Magallanes." When I redid the translation for the website of the Centro de Estudios Martianos in Havana a few years ago, though, I really felt it was necessary to include the accent because I've seen all too often how the word America leads to misreadings—many deliberate—as monolingual Anglophones assume it is synonymous with the United States and can only mean the United States.

In other words: América is not America is not the Americas. Sometimes an accent can be a geopolitical statement. There isn't

---

1. Several nations, including the United States, divide the earth's landmasses into seven continents, but many other places count six or fewer, with North and South America as a single entity. Not even that seemingly natural number is politically neutral.

one right way to approach this question of the accent, and there shouldn't be, just as there should be no pinnable, all-encompassing approach to what America is, no trans-historical shortcut for addressing cultural specificity. While the diacritic was essential to translating Martí's text at a certain moment and continues to generate important conversations, at this moment and in this context, we chose the more naked *America*. Our goal in selecting texts from across this vast expanse and uniting them under this rubric is to reclaim and redistribute the name *America*, fraught provenance and all, and to assert the plurality contained within its singular as a constellation rather than a consolidation.

MANIFESTO
ANTHROBSCENE

by KAREN TEI YAMASHITA *and*
RONALDO LOPES DE OLIVEIRA
art by RONALDO LOPES DE OLIVEIRA

Of learning to love our country, wherein we differ even
from… the inhabitants of Topinamboo.
—Jonathan Swift, *A Modest Proposal*, 1729

Tupi or not Tupi, that is the question.
—Oswald de Andrade, *Manifesto antropófago*, 1928

IT IS BEFITTING TO commemorate the 466th year since the Caeté
ate Bishop Pedro Fernandes Sardinha and some 30 of his compan-
ions. What a feast!

Clink glasses and make a hearty toast with vintage Bishop Sardinha:
Saúde!

When Pedro Álvares Cabral discovered Brazil for the Portuguese, on April 22, 1500, there were 11 million Indians in 2,000 tribes. Over the next 100 years, 90 percent of these people were wiped out.

For those who prefer the cocktail: the muddled balls of Cabral in lime and minty sugar doused in cachaça. Tim-tim.

In 1541, in search of El Dorado, Francisco de Orellana discovered the Amazon River, traversing it from Iquitos, on the Napo River, to its great mouth, on the Atlantic Ocean.

For appetizers, commence with Francisco de Orellana's right ear, wrapped in gold leaf and pickled with hints of guaraná, cinnamon, clove, and café.

In 1550, Hans Staden was taken prisoner by Jeppio Wasu and Alkindar Miri of the Tupinambá, brought to the coastal village of Ubatuba, and ritually prepared to be eaten.

Additionally, a French pâté of Hans Staden's left big toe and liver on a thin, carefully crafted tapioca crepe.

In 1799, Alexander von Humboldt encountered on the Orinoco River two Amazon parrots who continued to speak the dead language of the extinct Maipure people.

The first course might be a cabbage-and-manioc stew of the butt of Alexander von Humboldt.

From 1848 to 1859, Henry Walter Bates explored the Amazon from the Tocantins River to the Tefé River, in the upper Amazon, collecting 14,714 mostly insect species, 8,000 of which were said to be previously unknown.

An interlude, to cleanse the palate: a sorbet of the lymph nodes of Henry Walter Bates, laden with edible orchids.

In 1911, Theodor Koch-Grünberg traveled from Manaus, up the Rio Branco to Mount Roraima, documenting the legends of the Pemon people.

In 1928, Mário de Andrade published the novel *Macunaíma*, based on stories lifted from Theodor Koch-Grünberg's ethnographic narratives.

Second course: a spicy coconut–and–palm oil muqueca of the tender breast of Theodor Koch-Grünberg.

Percy Harrison Fawcett disappeared in 1925, while traveling from Cuiabá and crossing the upper Xingu River on an expedition to discover the Lost City of Z.

In 1952, the Kalapalo tribe returned what were believed to be Fawcett's bones to Orlando Villas Bôas, who brought them home to São Paulo in a box.

Accompany the muqueca with fluffy rice seasoned with peppery parts of Percy Harrison Fawcett.

In 1955, Claude Lévi-Strauss published *Tristes Tropiques*, an ethnographic analysis of the Amazonian people.

For dessert: a banana crème brûlée made with Claude Lévi-Strauss's spit.

The Amazon is not a multinational e-commerce marketplace.

The Amazon is not in the cloud.

To finish, an aperitif of the distilled brains of Jeff Bezos, accentuated by coconut beijinhos.

The Amazon rainforest is the living archive of 300 million years of Earth's genetic endowment.

The Amazon Basin occupies 40 percent of the South American continent.

To paradise, where saudade is eternal.

At 3.2 million square miles, the biogeographic Amazon can tuck itself into the 3.7 million square miles that contain the USA. Or, it is 12 times the size of Texas.

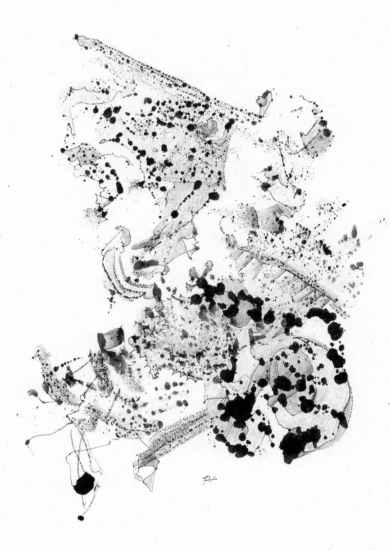

The Amazon River, which is 10 times more voluminous than the great Mississippi, can be 24.8 miles wide and discharges an average of 300,000 cubic feet per second of water into the Atlantic. The silt deposit at its mouth forms an island the size of Switzerland, named Marajó.

The Amazon produces half of its own rainfall, sharing this precipitation across South America as far south as Argentina.

How tasty, tasty was my ecotourist.

In 2019, more than 300,000 acres of the Amazon (172,000 soccer fields' worth of land) were cleared. In August, they were burned for agricultural conversion. On August 19, the skies over the city of São Paulo, more than 2,000 miles from the Amazon, turned black. That year, satellites located 70,512 fires across Brazil.

One in 10 known species on Earth lives in the Amazon.

Have you eaten your vegetable elite today?

The Amazon's richly diverse plant and animal ecosystem, both terrestrial and aquatic, has been maintained by Indigenous people for over 30,000 years.

The Amazon's matrimony and sustainability are in the care of tribal people.

Aí que preguiça!

Today, between 300 and 400 Indigenous tribes live in the Amazon, 50 of which do not have contact with the outside world.

The population of the 305 tribes of the Brazilian Amazon numbers 900,000, a scant 0.4 percent of Brazil's population.

The largest tribe within Brazil is the Guaraní, numbering 51,000, and very little land has been left to them. In the Amazon, some 26,000 Yanomami occupy more than 23 million acres.

The Ticuna number 40,000, and the smallest tribe consists of just 1 man.

The doctor recommends a settler colonoscopy every 50 years.

For 400 years, starting in 1501, almost 5 million enslaved Africans were transported to Brazil.

By the end of the sixteenth century, fugitives from slavery had established mocambo or quilombo communities, many hidden in the Amazon.

The largest quilombo, Palmares, numbered 20,000 people before it was invaded in 1694. Its leader, Zumbi dos Palmares, was killed on November 20, 1695.

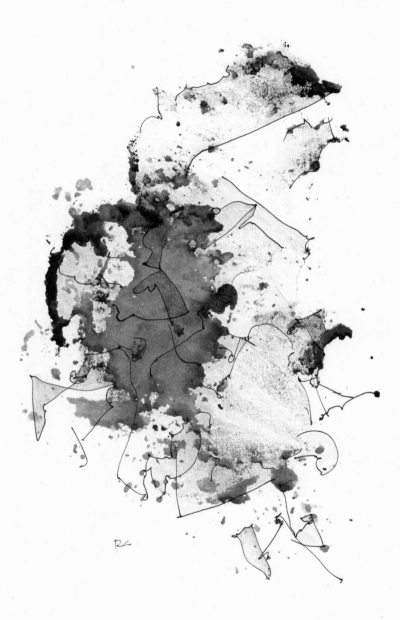

French Revolution tomorrow. Human rights for happiness the day before yesterday.

Brazil was the last country in the Americas to abolish slavery, which it did in 1888.

Eat, drink, and be carnaval, for tomorrow?

Three thousand contemporary quilombo settlements have been officially recognized since 1988, although half lack land titles. They are spread over 50 million acres, mostly in the Amazon.

Calculations of value: monocultures of livestock (Cain) versus soy (Abel) versus the sustainably managed forest (Eden).

Recycling what goes in, must come out.

Life in the Amazon's trees exists in 5 stories: floor, shrub, understory, canopy, overstory, each layer comprising a unique plant and animal ecosystem.

The Amazon, which hugs the equator, has two seasons, wet and dry, following Earth's north-south tilt toward the sun. The wet season is from December to May; the dry season is from June to November.

During the wet season, 6 to 12 feet of rain falls, and the Amazon River may rise 40 feet. In this season, forest life moves upward to the canopy.

There is no sin below the equator.

Technology must be employed to protect and preserve the unique Amazonian environment, to continue the study of its complex ecological systems, and to discover its rich and still-unknown biomedical resources.

You eat, therefore, you are.

To preserve the Amazon, its vast ecosystem and inhabitants, Earth's largest gaming reserve will be established.

Deforestation for cattle, sugar, and soy production will be permitted only outside the perimeters of the Amazon. While this may result in a scarcity of beef, ethanol, and tofu, the price of these commodities will rise.

The production and export of beef, sugar, and soy has never filled the stomachs of Brazilians.

Dieting for a small planet.

Timber, oil, and mineral extraction will cease within the boundaries of the Amazon. To compensate, Brazil will garner International Monetary Fund bartering credits, calculated to match losses amounting to trillions of dollars.

The rest of the planet will pay Brazil for the precious oxygen expelled by the capacious lungs of the Amazon.

Breathe in. Breathe out. Unite the mind with air.

A no-fly zone must be adopted to preserve the purity of the area and to prohibit all outside contact.

In addition to electronic fencing, satellite sensor technologies will be employed to secure the border, conduct surveillance, and to collect data.

As the Amazon biome is the single major preserve of Brazil, its security will depend on the strict coordination of and enforcement by the country's army, navy, and air force.

Capitalizing on the eternal prosperity of humanity.

A return to free, nomadic living over a great expanse of preserved land area will promote exercise and health.

Higher worth will be given to pure, Indigenous, non-contact peoples. For example, quilombolas will be regarded as having secondary value, considering their genealogy.

Toward the preservation of African cultures and histories of the enslaved.

The primary concern will be to produce a highly organic and pure native food source.

DNA testing can substantiate the purity of the species.
Sex or food? Food or sex? You choose.

Careful calibration of age, sex, weight, and body mass will involve a qualified team of doctors and researchers.

Optimal preservation of healthy bodies within a natural and original environment will create the most excellent model of health care on Earth.

Toward the preservation of Indigenous cultures.

To preserve the appropriate balance between and population of the tribes, artificial insemination may be employed.

Embedded-chip technology may not disturb or interfere with body art such as tattoos or piercings.

Gaming licenses will be granted through a high-stakes lottery; to enter, participants must pay a significant price.

A commission of researchers will convene yearly to decide on the appropriate hunting season, and on the number and selection of Amazonians for eating.

Strict regulations about how to hunt will be enforced. For example, no firearms will be allowed—only primitive methods: arrows, spears, darts, knives. Traps must be preapproved.

Save Indians by making them Indians again.

The kill must be clean so as to preserve the integrity of the meat.

Overhead drone and satellite filming will meticulously record the hunt.

Michelin-starred chefs will compete to craft the most sophisticated recipes. However, only 10 percent of these recipes may be based on foreign influences, defining a cuisine original to the Amazon, and initiating a study of Amazonian food sources.

The use and value of all body parts—hair, bones, blood, teeth, et cetera—will be carefully considered to ensure 100 percent consumption, zero waste.

Eat everything before you die.

A place at the table will be reserved only for high dignitaries. If 100 dignitaries are selected, they must be carefully culled to 10.

The rich matrimony of Amazonian plant life (fruits, roots, fungi, bulbs, palm, flowers, et cetera) and animal life (fish, birds, reptiles, monkeys, tapirs, et cetera), as well as their hallucinogenic and medicinal properties, should afford new avenues of culinary pleasure.

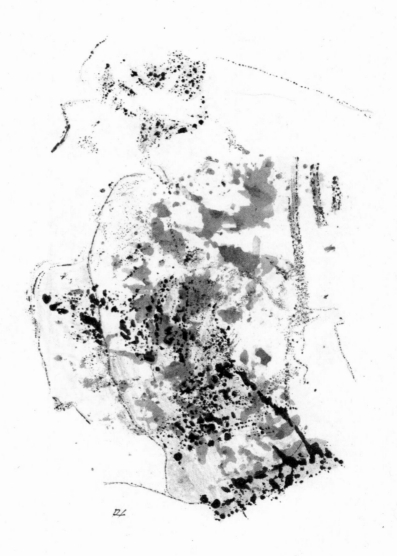

Save the Amazon.

Eat the noble savage.

WASHINGTON CHATEAUBRIAND SILVA (W.C.S)

IN THE 466TH YEAR

OF THE EATING OF BISHOP PEDRO FERNANDES SARDINHA

BIBLIOGRAPHY/BIOGRAFIA

Andrade, Mário de. *Macunaíma*. São Paulo: E. Cupolo, 1928.

Andrade, Oswald de. "Manifesto Antropófago." *Revista de antropofagia*. São Paulo, May 1928; Oswald de Andrade's "Cannibalist Manifesto." Translated by Leslie Bary. *Latin American Literary Review*, vol. 19, no. 38 (Jul.–Dec., 1991), pp. 35–37.

Haraway, Donna Jeanne. *Staying with the Trouble: Making Kin in the Chthulucene*. Durham, NC: Duke University Press, 2016.

Léry, Jean de. *History of a Voyage to the Land of Brazil.* Translated by Janet Whatley. Berkeley: University of California Press, 1990.

Lestringant, Frank. *Cannibals: The Discovery and Representation of the Cannibal from Columbus to Jules Verne*. Berkeley: University of California Press, 1997.

Portinari, Candido. *Portinari devora Hans Staden*. Edited by Mary Lou Paris and Ricardo Ohtake. São Paulo: Terceiro Nome, 1998.

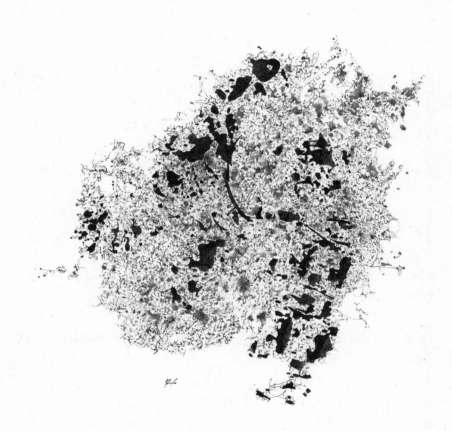

Smith, Amanda M. *Mapping the Amazon: Literary Geography after the Rubber Boom*. Liverpool: Liverpool University Press, 2021.

Staden, Hans. *Hans Staden's True History: An Account of Cannibal Captivity in Brazil (Warhaftige Historia und Beschreibung eyner Landtschafft der wilden, nackenten, grimmaigen Menschfresser Leuthen in der Newenwelt America gelegen)*. Translated and edited by Neil L. Whitehead and Michael Harbsmeier. Durham, NC: Duke University Press, 2008.

Swift, Jonathan. *Gulliver's Travels*, 1726.

Swift, Jonathan. *A Modest Proposal*, 1729.

Viveiros de Castro, Eduardo. *Cannibal Metaphysics*. Translated and edited by Peter Skafish. Minneapolis: University of Minnesota Press, 2014.

HUACO PORTRAIT

by GABRIELA WIENER
translated by GABRIELA JAUREGUI

THE STRANGEST THING ABOUT being alone here in Paris, inside this ethnographic museum in the shadow of the Eiffel Tower, is the realization that all these figurines that look like me were torn from the cultural legacy of my country by a man whose last name I share.

In the glass of the display case, my reflection blends with the contours of these brown-skinned characters, with eyes like tiny, simmering wounds, bronze noses, and cheekbones as polished as mine, until we form a single hieratic, naturalistic composition. For most people, a great-great-grandfather is little more than a vestige, unless he brought to Europe the trifling sum of four thousand pre-Columbian pieces, and his greatest feat is having not found Machu Picchu but having come close.

The Musée du Quai Branly is in the seventh arrondissement, in the middle of the eponymous quay, and it's one of those European museums that house large collections of non-Western art, from America, Asia, Africa, and Oceania. These are very pretty museums erected around ugly things. As if someone thought that by painting the ceilings with Australian Aboriginal designs and placing a bunch of palm trees in the halls, we would feel a little more at home and forget that everything here should be thousands of miles away. Including me.

To make the most of this work trip, I've come to visit Charles Wiener's collection. Every time I come into a place like this, I have to resist the urge to claim it all as mine and ask for everything to be returned in the name of the Peruvian state. This feeling grows stronger in the hall that bears my last name and that is full of anthropomorphic and zoomorphic figurines of different pre-Hispanic cultures thousands of years old. I try to find some kind of prospectus, something that will contextualize the pieces in time, but they're exhibited in a disconnected and isolated way, and labeled only with vague or generic inscriptions. I take several photos of the wall that reads "Mission de M. Wiener," much as I did when I went to Germany and noticed with dubious satisfaction that my name was everywhere. Wiener is one of those last names that are derived from place names, like Epstein, Aurbach, and Ginzberg. Some Jewish communities used to adopt the names of their towns and cities as a matter of attachment. Wiener is a German family name meaning "from Vienna." Like the sausages. It takes me a few seconds before I realize the "M." is the M in Monsieur.

Even though his scientific mission was typical for a nine-teenth-century explorer, I joke at friends' dinner parties about how my great-great-grandfather was a huaquero of international scope. No euphemisms required; I simply call those plunderers of archaeological remains huaqueros: people who still traffic in cultural and artistic goods today. They may be gentlemen pundits or mercenaries, and they may take ancient treasures to museums in Europe or to the living rooms of their criollo homes in Lima. The word *huaquero* comes from *huaca*, or *wak'a* in Quechua, meaning a sacred Inca site that, in general, ends up as an archaeological site or simply as a ruin. In their catacombs, communal authorities used to be buried next to their funerary offerings. Huaqueros systematically invade these spaces looking for tombs or objects of value, and leave a shit pile behind because of their less-than-professional methods. The problem is that their procedures do not allow for accurate studies of the sites afterward; they make it impossible to trace any sign of identity or cultural memory that might be used to reconstruct the past. And so huaquear is a kind of violence: it transforms fragments of history into private property, the props and decor of an ego. Hollywood makes movies about art thieves and huaqueros alike: their misdeeds are not exempt from glamour. Without going too far, Wiener has gone down in history not only as a scholar, but as the "author" of this collection of works, erasing their real and anonymous authors, and has been backed by the alibi of science and by the money of an imperialist government. Back then, moving dirt around was called archaeology.

I walk through the hallways of the Wiener collection, and among the displays full of huacos, one stands out because it's empty. In the reference I read: "Momie d'enfant," but there is no trace of it. Something in this blank space sets off an alarm in me. The fact that it's a burial. That it's the burial of an unidentified child. That the display is empty. That it is, after all, an open or reopened burial, infinitely desecrated, shown as part of an exhibit that tells the triumphant history of one civilization over others. Can the denial of the eternal rest of a child tell that story? I wonder if they've sequestered the little mummy to restore it, as one restores a painting, and if they've left the empty display in the hall as a wink to a certain avant-garde art. Or if the space it no longer occupies is a permanent indictment of its disappearance, as when they stole a Vermeer from a Boston museum and they left the empty frame hanging permanently, so no one would forget. I ponder the idea of theft, of relocation, of repatriation. If I didn't come from a land of forced disappearance, in which there are unburials and, above all, clandestine burials, perhaps that invisible burial behind glass wouldn't speak to me. But something inside of me insists—perhaps because the caption says that the absent child's mummy was from Chancay, on the central coast of Peru, in the department of Lima, which is also the city where I was born. My head moves through different imaginary mass graves, carved on the surface, as I plant my shovel in the hole of unreality and remove the dirt. This time, the reflection of my Incan profile doesn't blend with anything, and for a few seconds it's the only content, albeit spectral, in the empty display. My shadow trapped behind glass, embalmed and exposed, replaces the mummy, erases the border between reality and montage, restores it by proposing a new scenery for the interpretation of death: my shadow, washed and perfumed, empty of all organs, ageless, like a translucent piñata full of myrrh—nothing that the wild desert dogs could destroy and devour.

A museum is not a cemetery, though it's quite similar. Wiener's exhibit doesn't explain whether the child that isn't there was ritually sacrificed, murdered, or died of natural causes—or when or where. What's certain is that this place is not a huaca, or the top of a volcano where one can be delivered to gods and men so the harvest may be blessed and rain may fall as thick and constant as in myths, like a whirl of baby teeth and ruby grains of juicy pomegranates showering the cycles of life. Here, mummies are not as well preserved as they would be in snow.

Archaeologists say that in the high volcanoes of the extreme south, they have found the bodies of children who seem to be sleeping in graves of ice—that they're so well preserved that, when they see them for the first time, it seems as though they might wake up from their ancient slumber and start talking that very instant. And they're never alone. The Children of Llullaillaco, in the Andean cordillera, were buried together: Lightning girl, age five; the Boy, six; and the Damsel, fifteen. And together they were disinterred.

In not-so-remote ancient times, here in a European capital, children were also buried together in the same section of cemeteries, as if they were all siblings, or as if a pestilence had taken them all suddenly and they inhabited a sort of tiny ghost city inside the great city of the dead, so that if they woke in the middle of the night, they could all play together. Every time I visit a cemetery, I head to the kids' zone and read, between startles and sighs, the goodbyes their families have left in their mausoleums, and I start to imagine their frail lives and deaths, often caused by insignificant illnesses. In front of this empty child's sepulcher, I wonder whether the terror that a child's death elicits in us nowadays comes from that ancient fragility, and whether we've forgotten the custom of sacrificing them, the normality of losing them. I've never seen the graves of contemporary dead children. Who in their right mind would take the corpse of their child to a cemetery? You'd have to be crazy.

However, this tomb without a child, this child without a tomb not only has no siblings or playmates; now it's lost. If the child were there, I imagine someone—which would be me—giving in to the impulse to take the momie d'enfant in my arms, the baby huaqueada by Wiener, wrapped in a textile with two-headed snake designs and ocean waves bitten by time, then start running toward the quay, leaving the museum behind, heading toward the Eiffel Tower with no fixed plan other than to get as far away as possible from there, firing shots in the air....

The legend of my great-great-grandfather Wiener is that of a discreet German teacher turned Indiana Jones overnight.

In the homes of all the Wieners I know, there's this cheap black-and-white reproduction of the Austrian's surly face, framed and decorating some piece of furniture. They say the original had always been in the family and that one of my grandfather's sisters kept it until her death.

One of my uncles, the one they say looks most like him, became a historian, inspired by the feat of his great-grandfather, and was the only one who had seen Charles's book *Perú y Bolivia*. He'd come across a French edition in the 1980s in a Parisian bookstore, and had even thought of finding a way of publishing it in Peru. When the Spanish translation finally appeared, in 1993, he felt slightly chagrined because someone had beat him to it, but above all he was excited to finally be able to read the book.

On the night of the book launch in Lima, the translator was sitting with the consecrated novelist Edgardo Rivera Martínez, former Peruvian president Fernando Belaúnde, and other illustrious Peruvians in a show of certain cultural importance. Proud that Charles's legacy was finally being recognized, my family attended the event, and the organizers announced our presence to the audience.

"Tonight we have the pleasure of the company of Wiener's only descendants in our country," one of them said. They had no idea that Charles had had a son here and that we had multiplied, oblivious to his figure. We could've just as well been imposters, but they hadn't bothered to find out. In truth, we couldn't have proved anything. My family stood up proudly from their seats, feeling for the first time that our pompous, foreign-sounding last name was of some use.

In truth, beyond his photo in a display case or on a side table in our modest homes, Charles started to become well known in Peru as one of the first European scholars to confirm the existence of Machu Picchu, almost forty years before Hiram Bingham and *National Geographic* photographed the monument for the first time, uncovering its majesty for the world to see. In the black-and-white magazine images, the intense green of its mountains looked deep black, the Huayna Picchu summit surrounded by a stole of immaculate clouds, the watchtower intact, the three windows of heaven, the Intihuatana sundial telling time precisely. Charles was so close to that; in fact, he came the closest. At this point I always start to imagine my life as if I were the legitimate descendant of the "discoverer" of one of the Seven Wonders of the World, even though we all know what "discovering" America and everything that's always already been there really means. Would I have a pool in my house today? Could I ride the tourist train to the citadel for free? Could I claim my rights over those lands, as many have tried to do since 1911, when the gringo explorer came? Should I have signed my name on one of the granite walls of the Sun Gate, as did Agustín Lizárraga, the Cusquean civil servant in charge of bridges, who arrived in 1902, nine years before Bingham himself, only to immediately exit the stage of history in a punk, infantile gesture— as if to say: *If it weren't for my great-great-grandfather and his little map, you wouldn't be here taking a selfie?*

But Wiener didn't make it. Worse, he left clues in his maps and a very approximate location that helped Bingham to arrive, because of course one never knows whom one might be working for. "I was told of other cities, Huayna Picchu and Machu Picchu, and resolved to make one last excursion east, before continuing south," he writes of the detour that would take him to far less important ruins and that would definitely keep him from making the most extraordinary find in Peruvian history. To have come close and missed something by the skin of one's teeth has never been a good excuse. In fact, of all the facets of failure, this one is especially outrageous. And no one would want to claim it as their inheritance.

In his book, Wiener drew a precise map of the Santa Ana Valley with the indications that the locals gave him, which included landmarks and came very close to the real route, but he finally lost his way and didn't discover anything: he was unable to claim the medal for bumping into something that had been built centuries ago, to stake his flag and sing "La Marseillaise."

He didn't have the same luck as his great-great-granddaughter, who, in the late twentieth century, took a hit from an apple bong at the end of a trip and was filled with gratitude for the dazzling apparition, amid the fog, of the green and rocky Lost City of the Incas, after having climbed summits of almost sixteen thousand feet, walked for days down the long trails of the Sacred Valley, and crossed miles of forests on the Inca Trail, sleeping under the starry sky next to her best girlfriends, dying to touch their tits. Despite it all, we could affirm, without lying, that I got to Machu Picchu before Charles. I simply got there. And he didn't.

If I tried to write a similar synopsis of my life, of my current condition as an immigrant from a former Spanish colony now living in Spain, I'd have to add the bastard nature that the Franco-German scientific expeditions of the nineteenth century lend me—geopolitical movements that make me, at the same time, the descendant of a scholar and another archaeological or anthropological object.

We treasured the book for years, with its dozens of customs-and-manners plates of Indigenous life, and kept it untouched in a special place in our library. Every time I started to wander around its first pages, however, I shut it. I was horrified, incapable of reading it as the fascinating nineteenth-century travel chronicle that so many people find it to be. And I was especially incapable of avoiding its sentences about the savage Indians. Nothing about this character, lost in his violent and appallingly racist Eurocentrism, has anything to do with who I am, even though my family might glorify him.

I stopped thinking about the book for years. That tome, which left almost its real weight on my conscience, was back in Peru, and by then I was living on the other side of the Atlantic, even though sometimes, especially when the anecdote of the huaquero great-great-grandfather came up in conversation, the idea of not having read it would eat at me still: after all, I am a writer, and he's the only Wiener who has written a successful book.

We all have a white father. I mean, God is white. Or that's what we've been led to believe. The colonist is white. History is white and male. My grandmother, my mother's mother, called my father, her daughter's husband, "Mister," because she wasn't white but chola.[1] It was so strange to hear my grandma treating my father with that excessive and unwarranted respect. To her, my father was "Mister Raul."

When children in school called me "negra" as an insult, I found solace in holding his hand, so everyone would know that the slightly white man was my father—it made me less dark, less *insultable*. I suppose now that he's dead, what little whiteness was left in me has gone with him, even though I keep using his last name, and never my mother's, on everything I write.

For a long time, I thought the only whiteness I had was that last name, but my husband says my "human stain" is the opposite of Coleman's, the university professor in the Philip Roth novel of that title who wants to hide his Blackness. My brown identity, chola and sudaca,[2] tries to conceal the Wiener inside me.

---

1. Translator's note: It's important to note that in the Peruvian context, the words *chola* and *cholo* do not refer to the Mexican American urban subculture in US. As the author explains, "It's a term with colonial origins referring to a mestiza or mixed-race person but also occasionally to Indigenous people. Despite its colonial origins, today it's used in an extended way to refer to the Andean migrant in Lima or in other urban contexts and, increasingly, it has been reclaimed in a self-referential way."

2. *Sudaca* is a racist slur originating in Spain to refer to people of South American origin, many of them immigrants. Today the term has been reclaimed so that, as the author states, "many people call themselves sudaca as a form of pride and resistance."

Since I live in Spain, I constantly encounter people who say I have "a Peruvian face." What is a Peruvian face? The face of those women you see on the subway. The face in *National Geographic*. My great-great-grandmother Maria's face as seen by Charles.

My face is very similar to a huaco portrait. Every time I'm told this, I imagine Charles moving his brush over my eyelids to dust me off and estimate the year I was crafted. A huaco can be any piece of handmade pre-Hispanic ceramic, with diverse shapes and styles, painted delicately. It can be a decorative element, used in a ritual, or an offering in a burial. They're called huacos because they were found in sacred temples called huacas, buried next to important people. They can represent animals, weapons, or food. But of all huacos, huaco portraits are the most interesting. They are pre-Hispanic photo IDs. They are images of Indigenous faces, so realistic that for many, looking at them is like looking at ourselves in the mirror of time.

My favorite huaco are Mochica ceramics, the most sophisticated due to their capacity to thread narrative like three-dimensional comics or frame-by-frame sculptures. Like antiquity's TV. The Moche specialty were sculptures of beheading gods and erotic huacos, which were their porn, the Andean Kama Sutra. Fucking and chopping off heads: not much else in this life. My grandfather Felix, my mother's father, was born in that area on the northern Peruvian coast. That's why, the first time I showed my Spanish girlfriend a series of erotic huacos, she thought she could recognize me in the earthenware women who swallow penises larger than their own bodies, who orgasm, and who give birth to children on all fours.

There's something in this perverse mix of huaquero and huaco that runs in my veins, something that unhinges me...

I shut myself up with Charles's book, my family's bible, in which grandiose matters such as the past and history depend on the single gaze of someone who decides what to tell and what to omit, a sort of God. There are moments when our contradictory traveler is besotted by the magnificence of the Inca past, subjugated by the remains of their architecture, and makes an effort to capture the complexity of present-day Peruvians. There are others when he wallows in slander.

In one passage, Wiener refers to Peruvians as people with an "unwholesome" and "abusive constitution," and in whom one can find "the pernicious causes for the mummification of this people and the degradation of the individual." Of autochthonous Indigenous peoples, he says, "They didn't know how to die, this is why the Indians don't know how to live." He then gives a cruel description of the cycle of their lives: "as a child he knows no happiness; as a teenager, enthusiasm; as a man, honor; as an old man, dignity."

"A visionary," my husband tells me via chat, and we laugh like Nazis because we refuse to be offended. It would be too easy. Because Charles judged these "vile mummies"—disinterred by Spaniards, or Austrians, or Frenchmen, or Austrians who longed to be Frenchmen—from the viewpoint of his own topography. But we judge ourselves ironically, as we know ourselves to be the product of that confrontation.

Wiener's viciousness is so grotesque, it's laughable. If he had talent for one thing, it was for insult, I say. And that, by the way, is something one does inherit. There are writers who give back beauty to the world and there are those who scream its ugliness. If there are only those two possibilities, Wiener is not a writer, I tell myself; he's the troll to an entire civilization.

I don't know why I'm undertaking this ritual, what I seek in an external observer's gaze, that of a fucking Americanist. But then, without great enthusiasm, I reach a well-told passage that hooks me. As Charles is on his way to Puno and passing through a ranch called Tintamarca, the ranch owner suggests that he should take an Indian back to give European scholars an idea of this race. Wiener answers that procuring an Indian, even more so an Indian child, is very hard; he's been trying for several days to get one of them to follow him, but it's proved impossible. The man suggests he should buy one: "Give some coins to a poor Indian woman dying of thirst and who is starving her child, I'm talking about a horribly alcoholic Indian. In exchange, she will give you her little one. Moreover, you'll be doing good." Wiener goes to look for the woman and her child. He asks the boy's name and she replies, "Juan." He asks him if he has a father, and she answers no in Quechua. "Very few times have I witnessed such a repellent spectacle," writes Wiener. "This mother, still young, gnawed at by all possible vices, and the little being who had no other clothes except a poncho that barely reached his waist. I made up my mind." He woke the mother, who was sleeping, and "effected the projected 'gift' exchange. I exhorted the child to say goodbye to his mother; he seemed not to understand what I was asking; but the mother understood well enough and with her hand shaking from alcohol, she made the sign of the cross on her child. I shuddered in disgust at witnessing such blessing of vice; placed the little one on a mule.... And off we went. Little Juan understood, and he then thought himself obliged to cry out. I asked him what he wanted. Do you think he asked to be brought back to his mother's side and not to leave his land and keep being the savage he was? Not at all: he asked me for liquor!"

I down a big gulp of Coca-Cola. The bubbles hurt my throat like little knives, and I read the passage a second time but out loud. When I do, my voice sounds shriveled, unrecognizable. I'm stupefied. Wiener bought an Indigenous child off his mother on the road. He not only deprives her of the boy but brutalizes her in his own mythological tale of the white savior. He strings together the legend of his own superior goodness while turning the possibility of aid into violence and narcissistic affirmation. Blaming the mother, of course, has always worked to perpetrate child robbing, whether it's done by a father, a democratic state, or a dictatorship, whether in American border cages or by taking custody away from migrant mothers who arrive on European coasts. As if making children cross the sea or the desert were a maternal death-drive and not about life. As if the ragged hangover of that Indigenous mother had not come after the power-binge of those bearded men on beasts. And, further, Wiener manages to dedicate to her some insults inspired by disgust.

I had never heard of a child bought—or, I should say, stolen—by Wiener. I don't know why my uncle the historian or my father never mentioned it, and it's not in any of the biographies I can get hold of. It's barely a footnote on one of the pages describing his long voyage. They didn't know, or it didn't matter to them. Juan's sole existence, hypothetical or real, unleashes a rain of images of possible lives, mine and others'.

In his book, Charles tells of how they came back from Puno to Cusco, how when a train passed he realized, admiringly, that Juan had never seen one in his life and started describing it in a Quechua sentence that he translates as "this street that moves and fumes." I repeat several times the sentence that made the European man fall in love, and imagine Juan, in his colorful poncho, walking inside a train as if he were on a moving street that puffs smoke signals, his hand in the hand of the man who distances him from metaphors.

Touched by the child's candor and ignorance, according to Wiener's own confession, he decides to take Juan to Europe, to France, to find out whether he might overcome his barbarity if he were raised far from the Indigenous world. "Since then," writes my great-great-grandfather in his travelogue, "I've closely followed the child's moral and intellectual development. He now understands French and makes himself understood. He's very intelligent and what's commonly known as well-educated. He's proven to me that, to progress, this race needs nothing more than example and teaching."

Juan is not a piece of ceramics to be extirpated from the rubble; he's not gold or silver; he's not a rickety mummy of a child to be exhibited in a museum far from the volcanoes. But he does travel among the scholar's belongings when he crosses the pond. He's a scrap of the small part Wiener played in the transformation of what is known in Europe as history. He's a part of his *mission*, which is not that of a conqueror or a discoverer but of a scientific voyager who seeks to "light the sun of the Inca, brutally extinguished by the Spanish cross, once again." If there's an état d'âme that travels across his book, it's one of incredulousness upon seeing the glorious past built by these people mutated into this "paltry, impoverished, small" world. Because they "were annihilated, judged and condemned as barbarians." This is why, in his notes, Wiener assures his readers that he has entrusted the collections gathered on his mission as "goods belonging to him" to the French state, so much more humanist and enlightened than the brutish Spaniards. Juan is also a good for Europe.

In 1877, we were approaching the twentieth century, and my family member could not help but civilize everything in his path.

I close the book. It has so many pages, it makes a noise as it falls to one side, exhaling its years, as if an old man had blown his bad breath on my face. Did Juan have eyes as small and fiery as mine when he saw all this for the first time? It's strange. I know I have Charles's blood in my veins, but it's the adoptee who feels like kin to me.

My grandfather took an Indigenous boy to put him in a vitrine, as they did with King Kong. They say "Indians" who were taken to Europe did not survive long. I've been here fifteen years already and it seems like a miracle.

COLORSCAPE (MUSÉE DU LOUVRE, 2019)

by LAIA JUFRESA

A GONG BANGS ONCE, twice, three times. The crowd hushes. This is a walk-through space, its usual function to connect the subway to the galleries. One of the museum's main digestive tubes: eat a tourist up, push it out the other end. A space reserved for shuffling, for disposing of coats and searching through bags and pockets, and which has never once sat still during the daytime, or at least not since its latest archaeological disturbance, in 1983, but which now suddenly freezes. Silence spreads through the long corridor like lava, a righteous sizzling in its wake. This—these many people going quiet, standing codo a codo in the museum's entrails—would in itself make for a great performance. But people didn't queue for hours just to pose as themselves. They are consumers, eager to be consumed. Here for the show, all of them. And after three more gong bangs, the show finally begins to creep up on them.

It starts with doubt. A shift so small they can't be sure this is it. Those more acquainted with the artist's work say it is, say, "This is it," and point to the floor, and peek between their feet to better see. Four hundred humans looking down at once, like synchronized ducking ducks. The floor, a nondescript gray tiled floor, is indeed changing. Slowly. It's hard to tell exactly when it happened, but now the floor is purple. And it begins to rise. Their feet are burgundy. It is a slow, dry flood. Their calves are pink, they'd like to touch the rich hue but are so close together that bending down isn't an option, so instead they make their necks long and perch down. Four hundred flamingos. Delighted, all of them.

The color rises. Their knees are violet, their thighs are aqua. Teal crotches, all of them, green bellies. Their torsos are orange, ochre, brown, their chests are red. Their necks are red. Their faces are red. Their bodies, too, now. They are all red. If they smile, their teeth are red, only the smiles are fading now. The impression of blood is too strong. Discomfort spreads through the room. A vague sense of organs, of vulnerable insides exposed: it makes them all crave armor. Now they're sorry they came, sorry they agreed to lock their phones away. It is a massacre they've willingly signed up for. They could die here. They stir. Someone weeps. The guards, until now fully taken in by the spectacle, tense and prepare to get to work if panic settles in. The red shakes and shimmers, it is burning them. Even if they close their eyes, it is still there, they can't unsee it. They can't escape it. The red is in them. They want to get out. All of them. Out of the red, out of the room, and out of themselves. And then, suddenly, they are. They are out.

They are gone.

Four hundred humans, gone in a swoop.

Gone.

Swallowed by darkness. Not the kind you get used to, either, but a total absence of light. In her little room atop it all, the artist steers. This is her moment. This is when she takes what she cannot give. She's plunged them into the gone and plans to bring them back. A miracle that they, and she, will soon have forgotten. But first she wants to appreciate it. And they, they do not know any of this. Silence erodes. The darkness is a state so disorienting that they all need to touch something. Their partner's arm, their own stomach, their face: *Still here*, says sweaty palm to sweaty front. Four hundred humans gone, buried alive, yet relieved to be out of the red, all of them, out of the fire: gone and turning to ashes. Will they be remembered? And then they remember.

The darkness brought some screams, but after a few seconds order settles in. Museumgoers. Art appreciators. Rule followers. This part always makes the artist nervous. Will it go wrong? Will people stand the pause? It is sixty seconds long and people have been instructed to keep quiet. It is the first rule in the briefing they received upon entering the museum tonight: "When darkness comes, please be quiet. We will have a minute of silence for the disappeared. For the abyss each leaves behind. And for those who have then fallen into those cracks. Can you hold them all in your mind for this dark minute? The dead and their living and those who are neither alive nor dead but in between. The desaparecidos. Please hold them all."

Silence. Long.

And then a few drops.

When color returns, it is in drips and drops.

They seem spare and random at first. White. Bluish. So soft. A breath of air, something like hope. Like all invisible things breaking into song.

And slowly the rain sound drops, the light drops increase in frequency and intensity, as if somehow the rain is getting closer. A hum, a thump, a roar. A waterfall. People gasp, some laugh. It is actual footage, projected onto the massive walls. Footage of the waterfalls of Tolantongo, Hidalgo. A series of caves, a maze of cascades. A massive, dripping, raw stone vagina, basically. The artist smiles from her little window. She still remembers the very first time she set foot there, and she remembers thinking about the painting *L'origine du monde*, and she remembers thinking, *This* is where the world begins.

There is a blue period to the piece, an oceanic descent. Cobalt. Navy. Prussian. Midnight. Interrupted here and there by a few brick-colored creatures that fade to an off-white shade and then to brick again. (Those who know them will know: An octopus. Another one.) There is a brief, irking yellowing of it all that again makes people first high, then quickly on edge. There is a calming, eerie moment when the hall, and everyone in it, turns sepia. Nostalgia floods them, all of them, even those born long after Technicolor. Then, slowly, the sepia is drained of its red undertones. It goes beige. It goes sand. Here and there a spiky burst of sage or olive green pops up. Sand and cacti: the desert. And from the arid ground spring, one by one, simple wooden crosses painted bright pink. Campo Algodonero, remembrance for the many women killed every day in

Mexico. Then each cross begins to twirl and twist, faster and faster, until they dissolve into something like ghosts, something like souls: exotic, angry butterflies, going fast, wildly flying, crashing methodically, hitting the audience on the chest. Then flying away. Up and away. Four hundred sets of cervical spines, seven vertebrae each, react as if on a spring mechanism: necks fold backward, eyes follow the dancing brushstrokes as they convene on the roof, twirl once more, then settle into a massive field of flowers, all colors, hanging upside down as if seen by bats settling to sleep. Softly swaying in the breeze. The crowd can't help it: they raise their hands like little children, they want to touch. They are like bees drunk on nectar as a sweet perfume is released through the hall. Then the flowers dry and fall and there is a communal sobering up in the prolonged, peaceful green section that closes the night, not with a bang but with a sad, understated graying of it all because the green is dying, everyone knows that.

This ending, an unresolved chord, divides the art critics but apparently not the French audience: the applause goes on for so long she almost opens her little door to either bow for them or shoo them away. But she does neither. Instead she shakes her folded arms like a hen attempting to take off and fly, in order to get some air to her damp armpits. She didn't *feel* nervous, but there you go, it never gets easier.

When the light comes back into the hall, it happens so slowly no one really notices. Like dawn breaking. Like growing up. Each person reencounters their own thoughts, they turn and greet their loved ones as if they hadn't seen them for some time, because indeed they've been on a journey. Some are perturbed, others peaceful, most are ready for dinner. They advance slowly, the hall restored to its usual proceedings. They shuffle along like penguins. The hallway can lead them to one of two sides. They do not know, none of them, that their final impression of the piece will depend on whether they go toward the subway or the pyramid.

Those who go for the metro come upon a series of seven plaques. Each states simply: MUSEOGRÁFICA, 1983. They probably won't even notice them, the artist knows, certainly won't have it in them to understand what they mean, but she is paying a historic debt to her country and her mentor. A public scratch for a private itch, really, but when has art ever been above that?

Those leaving through the Napoleon Hall, on the other hand, are in for a more obvious treat. As they emerge from the glass pyramid and come upon the main open-air courtyard, the humans notice the fountain. Or at least they notice other humans noticing it, and they stop in their tracks like a dog when it spots a squirrel. And, like dogs, they blink, tender and confused: Is this real or in their eyes only? Has the color so inhabited them that they can't shake it? Are their pupils still dilated?

Their pupils are still dilated. But they aren't imagining anything. The water has been dyed and appears to be a shade between crimson and purpurin, depending on the angle and the jests and the cultural references of each. Some will see agua de jamaica, others wine or blood. Some will see beauty, is all. Few will care to inquire. The fact is, the water in the main fountain of the Musée du Louvre has been dyed with cochineal. It took about two kilos of bugs. Around three hundred thousand dead beetles. Brought from Mexico in her handbag, then ground in small batches on her hotel room desk, using the back of the telephone handset, then mixed with the alum mordant in a ziplock bag. On the report she had to write for the Ministère de la Culture, though, before she was allowed to mess with the almost-sacred, full-of-limescale water of Paris, she specified: "Carmine. Natural dye derived from Oaxacan cochineal. Insects collected, dried and sanitized locally, then pulverized by Zapotec hands in a pre-Hispanic mortar and pestle."

THE
HUNGER ARTISTS

by CARLOS MANUEL ÁLVAREZ
translated by JULIA SANCHES

THE FRONT DOOR SNAPPED like a fractured bone, making the sound of misery. The natural fibers of the wood splintered, and the two leaves, timidly fastened with a lock and chain, came down. Like an artisanal SWAT team—less equipped and more disorganized, imitating the choreography of a Hollywood movie—over a dozen men and women from the Cuban security forces entered the headquarters of the San Isidro Movement, on Calle Damas 955 in Old Havana, disguised as health care workers, and forcibly detained the fourteen people who'd spent the past eight days protesting the arbitrary detention of one of their members, Denis Solís. Solís had been charged with contempt and sentenced by summary judgment to eight months in prison for calling a police officer who'd entered his home without his permission a "*penco* [coward] in uniform," filming the altercation, and uploading it to social media.

Helmed by Luis Manuel Otero, the San Isidro Movement is a tentacular organization whose nondenominational calling and amphibian nature make it difficult to classify. The group is composed of rappers from the slums, professors of design, dissident poets and playwrights, artists, scientists, and everyday people who have come together to fight the government's censorship of artistic expression in Cuba. The collective has transcended its own artistic identity, pushing citizens of various ideological backgrounds, experiences of exile, and sentimental educations to reimagine Cuba—not as a miserable, cursed, ridiculous place but as a country, something that deserves to be saved.

Five of the protesters were on hunger strike. I'd been there for less time than the others, but the two nights I spent at the sit-in were both exhausting and extraordinary. In fact, my unexpected arrival was being used by law enforcement as an excuse to perpetrate violence. "We don't want to have to do it this way," they said as a formality before breaking down the door. "This is how you always do it," we answered. I had just arrived from abroad and they were trying to charge me with violating COVID-19 health protocols, in spite of the fact that at noon on November 24, 2020, I'd gone straight from the airport to the site of the protest, where I had remained in isolation probably longer than any other passenger on my flight, or any of the people who'd entered Cuba since the country had opened to international travel nine days earlier.

There are those who believe I managed to sneak into Damas 955 because the police hadn't expected me to try. There are those who believe that the secret police were aware of my plans, of my trip from New York via Miami, and that they let me in without a fight because they planned to use it to their advantage. I still don't know what happened and doubt I ever will. Sometimes the surveillance machine is so incompetent that it becomes effective, and sometimes it's so effective that it becomes incompetent, but it always has the final word. Either way, the protesters at Damas 955 knew I was coming and deemed my presence necessary. Every decision that followed was made together, with a single goal in mind.

On the evening of November 25, public health officials got word to me that my COVID test at the airport had come back compromised or indeterminate—not positive—and that I would have to take another test before midnight at the polyclinic on Fifth and Sixteenth, in the neighborhood of Miramar. If I didn't, they would come and get me. The authorities weren't able to inform me directly, because by that point the telecom company had disconnected my cell phone, just as it had done to the cell phones of everyone else at the protest. Our ability to stay connected to the internet can only be described as an act of magic. The propaganda machine had started fabricating a political case before any medical proof was found, accusing me of noncompliance with public health protocols.

I found myself at a crossroads that turned out to not be a crossroads at all. If I left the house, I could be diagnosed with COVID-19. Then, using the possibility of contagion to break up the protest, the authorities would make it look like I'd slipped through the police cordon with help from the regime, as one of its pawns.

That kind of suspicion can permanently damage the moral integrity of any Cuban. It also happens to be one of the government's favorite, most effective strategies: infiltrating the collective conscience, making it seem like it's in more places than it actually is, which in turn ensures its wide reach; getting everyone to suspect the person next to them at the drop of a hat, so they're constantly hurling unfounded accusations at each other. Particularly effective is the way this logic of control hinges on its bad reputation, how its capital comes from its own disrepute. Those in power know they can destroy a person's credibility simply by convincing others that he or she belongs to them.

My other option, the one I was leaning toward, was to stay in San Isidro even if it meant the authorities would come and get me—and get the others, too, while they were at it. I felt like a nuisance and thought maybe I'd made a mistake by coming, but earlier that day, Luis Manuel Otero had told me that people were his reason for living and that he'd decided to end his seven-day thirst strike—which is much more harmful than a hunger strike—because of the support the group had received from abroad, because I'd flown all the way from New York, and because it was clear from the constant gestures of concern from his fellow protesters that they wanted him to stop, even as they respected his position. Otero, along with Maykel Osorbo, was the only one to put his body through that kind of physical punishment. His decision to end his thirst strike was more than just a response to his physical body's final, desperate cry; it seemed to come from a process of reflection.

"Is there a difference between a hunger strike and a thirst strike?" I asked, squatting beside him. Otero was lying on a thin mattress, wearing only a rag tied around his waist. The image reminded me of *Saint Paul the Hermit* by José de Ribera. Except this time the hermit was Black, marginalized.

"The difference is huge," he said. "You watch your body wither from the inside, your skin starts to hang loose. I'd put my feet in water—"

"Why?"

Sometimes, Otero explained, he would sit in a chair in a corner of the house, feet in a basin, elbows propped on his thighs, head lowered.

"I'd get the urge to, but then at a certain point I didn't want anything touching me anymore—not a shower, nothing. It was refreshing. I don't know—it felt good. My body was wasting away. You feel exactly how important water is, what it means. Seventy percent of your body is water, and you watch yourself dry out, literally. That's why I put my feet in water. I felt the wetness on my skin and it played tricks on my mind. But that only goes so far. You're not a plant sucking up water through your feet."

Otero's expressive black eyes became agile again after he drank water, offsetting his ghostliness and giving his disintegration a second wind. Hunger had chiseled his angular cheeks, chipping away at them minute by minute, like a portrait in bone.

"How did you feel right before you ended your thirst strike?"

"Nausea, stomach pain. Things start eating away at each other. The muscles, but especially the organs. I slept like a log the night before. As if my body were saying: *Sleep, man, get some rest. We're done fighting each other. Go on.* That night, I dreamed. I don't remember much, except that I was in a building with someone I knew. I could've gone another two days, or at least one."

Now and then, when he felt cold—the kind of cold only a person on a hunger or thirst strike can feel at the end of November in

Havana—he'd wrap a white sheet around his body. Maybe a thirst strike could be defined as a winter fever.

We were quiet for a moment. Then Otero continued:

"Sure, I could've pretended to drink a mouthful of water, but this isn't a performance. It's real life. I could've drunk a mouthful of water and filmed it. But another thing that happens is that your low energy starts to infect everyone around you."

"That's when you decided."

"My organs had started saying, *Look, I can't work as well as this other one anymore.* My feet got up and walked, but it was just mechanical. My heart said: *I'm on my own now. I need to fight for myself.* These are the images I have in my head. Your organs strike out on their own, and each one of them says: *Hold on. First I've got to save myself.* It's the kidney versus the liver, this one versus that one. But when you come back to reality, everything is connected, and one thing takes over another."

I pictured Otero's worn-out organs inside his withered body, feebly struggling against one another, sweltering under the sun of his political resolve.

"And what else?" I asked.

"Then there's death, our relationship with it. I'm not scared of dying. Death is just another state of being. For me, life is more complicated than death. The need to give your life meaning, to put some gas in it and make sure it keeps moving forward. I remember Yasser sitting there, looking at me. He's a chill, easygoing guy, but he was staring at me wide-eyed like, *Fuck, man, you're on your way out.*"

Yasser Castellanos was on hunger strike for thirty hours before the vomiting started. An extremely peaceful man, Yasser is a vegan and an animal rights advocate. During the sit-in, he spent hours meditating, spoke slowly in whispers, and composed a few lines of hip-hop. He looked exactly like the ceramic Buddhist monk that sat on the altar by the front door, beside an imposing Saint Barbara, a merciful Saint Lazarus, and a Mexican La Catrina, among other icons I couldn't place. He seemed like he was at a Tibetan retreat, not in the thick of a political uprising.

The protest was almost Babelian in composition, but despite this and the stress of the police cordon, Damas 955 brought together a flutter of different voices and inflections that found mutual ground in the movement and unity in being fed up with the government. There was a playful chaos to our interactions, and our shared sense of justice fostered an affection between us. I felt like I was at a public boarding school again, subject to the laws of a precarious but altruistic environment.

We showered and flushed the toilet with buckets of water from a cistern. We hung our clothes out to dry on cables in the backyard, next to a side wall. Those who weren't on hunger strike had to eat far from those who were, boiling their food and barely seasoning, it to avoid creating any temptation or suffering. Every corner of the house and the spaces under the stairs were cluttered with junk. Upstairs, a chicken pecked at whatever it could find among the mess, having transformed into a different kind of creature, like a cyborg hen. We slept on top of sheets on the concrete floor. The cracks in the bathroom tiles looked like irrigated furrows, and you could see the bricks and the thick, rusted pipes through the busted-up wall.

With wide, unfinished rectangular columns at its center, the modest home resembled a warehouse abandoned to an endless hunger strike, and this was part of its strength. The house spoke of a particular moment in time. Otero's cell phone didn't even have a case, its battery and wires exposed; it's no easy task for a political system to discipline a boy who is happy to live with a phone like that.

"Look at this," one of us would quip whenever we lacked something essential. "And they say we've sold out to imperialism!" Another thing we often joked about, though it may seem contradictory, was the prospect of living together at San Isidro after the regime had met our demands. But then Otero would lift his head and say he had no intention of seeing any of us again, once all this was over. Serious political struggles are not approached with solemnity or melodrama.

Esteban Rodríguez, a young man with asthma and an abundance of charisma, ended his hunger strike moments before the raid. Visibly uncomfortable and worn-out, he rested his elbows on the kitchen table and said: "I need to eat something." "Okay," the others answered. "You'll have to start with soup. Or we can make you some mashed taro." This frustrated Esteban, who was a bit overweight. "What?" he said with a sigh. "Not soup, no way. Give me a steak or something. I know what I need, and it isn't soup!"

Abu Duyanah Tamayo—a stocky, affable Muslim who'd been standing watch at the door after a neighbor attacked Otero, hurling bottles through the windows a few days earlier—could be seen either rolling out his prayer mat in a corner or lying in front of the only fan in the house. Anamely Ramos, a former professor at the Instituto Superior de Arte, who'd been fired from the university for authoring supposedly disrespectful articles and expressing critical opinions in front of high-ranking officials, mixed her Catholic inclination with a knowledge of African art and a devotion to gods from the Yoruba pantheon. In turn, when I asked Omara Ruiz, a wise and direct woman, if she was Catholic, she snapped: "Roman Catholic, please."

Osmani Pardo, who runs a private business as a "vendor and manufacturer of party goods and more," shared certain traits with Yasser Castellanos. He spoke little, choosing his words with care, and his face showed a deep kindness. Due to his practical knowledge and astonishing handiness, he was able to fix several of the house's many technical imperfections. I watched him build a resistor out of two cans and three wood pegs in a matter of minutes. His hands *thought*, not only because they could solve problems but because they were dexterous even when there was nothing to fix. In his spare time, Osmani quietly made a tree out of a tangle of copper wire, calling it "the tree of freedom."

Maykel Osorbo, a rapper, spoke the language of the ghetto and dropped pearls like "What if life is doubting the nonserious?" The poet Katherine Bisquet penned a few lines about San Isidro:

Inside hunger.
Inside a mo(ve)ment.
Inside a single scar
Stitched from belly button to breast.
I no longer fear night.
Make some mushroom pizza for me to eat tomorrow.
I want to taste freedom.

Completing the group were Adrián López, a sleepwalking eighteen-year-old with a nasal voice who'd dodged his military service; Jorge Luis, twenty-one, an expert in the science of getting online in Cuba; Iliana Hernández, a marathon runner and freelance journalist from Guantánamo who'd grown pale after days on hunger strike; and Angell, a small, discreet, almost frightened-looking mother of three who had lost her home. As if this group weren't diverse enough, I should note that on the day I arrived, Oscar Casanella—forced out of the Instituto Nacional de Oncología y Radiobiología for his political ideas—abandoned the strike as well as the site of the protest.

As soon as everyone agreed I should stay, a heightened sense of kinship enveloped us, the kind that pervades groups under siege. My arrival came with certain benefits: it would help us have a wider impact in the media and once again expose the forces of repression for what they really were.

On the evening of November 26, hours before the end, Omara Ruiz told me that, in a way, we were winning. It felt like an arm being wrapped around my shoulders. It's hard to explain why we thought we were winning, in light of what happened, but she was right. Her words were spoken in an enclosed space. The walls around us kept reality at bay.

Omara had taught at the Instituto Superior de Diseño but was fired for her work as a human rights activist. In a way, she was the one responsible for organizing our daily lives at the sit-in, calmly setting many of the guidelines we would follow.

Around eight that night, three Cuban security officers disguised as health care workers came to get me. The man who spoke with me sounded wooden, as law enforcement officers often do. Every profession has its specific vocabulary and body language. My parents are doctors, and a quick comparison erased any doubts I had about those men's identities, if I'd had any doubts at all. Doctors save lives; police officers cut them short. As we told the officers to leave, we realized a sizable operation was already set up outside: various patrolmen, two police vans, a crowd prepared with protest chants. This is when they shut down Facebook, Instagram, and YouTube across most of Cuba, not allowing access till almost an hour later.

They were nervous men and women. "When're they going to take me?" Esteban wondered after several officers walked past without touching him. Two guys grabbed hold of me. They dragged me stumbling down the stairs and then each pulled me in their direction. I almost crashed into one of the columns. I think their inexperience might have made them more dangerous. They didn't hit us; they tried to humiliate us. They led us by the neck or grabbed us by the arm; they didn't walk us in a straight line; they shoved us this way and that.

That's when I lost track of the three women in our group. Supposedly, the aim of the raid was to prevent the spread of the virus, but they carted the men to the Cuba and Chacón police station on Avenida del Puerto, and kept us locked in the police van for more than two hours, arms and legs entwined in the cubist darkness. The door was opened only occasionally, for the sake of Esteban's asthma.

Otero and Maykel Osorbo referred to themselves as runaway slaves. This gave San Isidro a historical awareness that the regime chose to ignore. Otero and Osorbo are Black, poor, and displaced. They live in precarious housing surrounded by luxury hotels designed for white-calved tourists. They are everything the revolution promised to fight for and instead persecuted, hunting them down in order to hide them from sight.

As the protagonist of Kafka's "A Hunger Artist" takes his final breaths in his cage at the circus, he asks for forgiveness. Only the supervisor, who has his ear to the cage, hears him (who else, if not the supervisor, would hear him?). "Of course," he says, "we forgive you." All the hunger artist has ever wanted is to be admired for resisting the temptation to eat, and when the supervisor says that they do admire him, the hunger artist responds that they shouldn't, because he had no choice but to fast; he couldn't do otherwise. And why? Well, because he could never find food that was to his taste. His last words are "If I had found it, believe me, I would not have caused a stir, and would have eaten my fill, like you and everybody else."

The men and women protesting at San Isidro were a bit like the hunger artist. They searched all over Cuba for food that was to their taste, wanting to be sated like everyone else, but turned up nothing. Which is why—since the only place they could find freedom was within—they began to eat themselves.

FLAT EARTH SOCIETY

by SOPHIE BRAXTON

PEOPLE WHO SPEND MORE time looking in the mirror have prettier facial expressions. We watched Aviela practice in the bathroom. We laughed at her, but we envied her perfect, pitiful frown. In the darkness, you shone a flashlight up at your face and told ghost stories about beautiful children who were trampled to death by overenthusiastic admirers. Nobody ever told us not to put plastic bags over our heads, so we did—but then I couldn't see you, and I couldn't breathe either. It seemed to me that one resulted from the other.

Where did you get those worried wrinkles? As soon as I was old enough to know that big walls are not made of moss but of the stone that the moss grows on top of, I wondered that. When I asked you, you went to the kitchen and returned red-eyed and sniffling.

It pained me, you know, to see your bird's nest hair empty of its aviary warmth.

Time passed quickly. I surpassed you in height. Our mothers stared differently at us, and stopped coming home. I grew dizzy from looking around for you. When I turned fourteen, I started working.

You didn't agree with my wanting to work. You said I should concentrate on school.

But it seemed wrong for an able-bodied person's work to consist entirely of remembering the dates on which ancient battles took place. Of standing up and sitting down and being quiet when snapped at.

I tired not from schoolwork but from wondering why.

When you saw that I could not be dissuaded, you told me I should ask around. *How old are you?* was always the first question. Then, *There's a nice little place that's hiring on the corner there.* Corners were so often spoken of that I doubted the existence of a center.

It was always foggy, and I wondered how we didn't suffocate or flatten beneath those clouds, when clouds are said to weigh one million pounds. I tried to climb above the fog, but even magnolia trees sagged under the bulk of my body. You stuck your head out the door and watched me silently.

Boys grew their hair long to attract girls through a sense of solidarity. I cut mine short in protest. Other children learned to hold cigarettes between the appropriate two fingers. You offered me one and I refused.

First I threaded eyebrows and did hair at a place where no one spoke English. Customers came to me with photographs on copy paper, stripes on the thing from a running-out printer. They knew who they wanted to look like: celebrities. After I finished, there was a noticeable disappointment as they stared in the mirror—that their faces had not shifted. No significant event had taken place. Pangaea remained intact, dumb with ancient grief.

When I handed in my uniform, I told my bosses, *When I thread clients' eyebrows, we're breathing into each other's mouths. I feel phantom pains! If Miss Garcia's knee hurts, so does mine. It happens when it rains. She told me that last week, but I already knew it.* I shook my head sadly, fat wobbling around my cheeks. Everybody always said I looked twelve—now I'm eighteen and they think I look twenty. *The backs of their necks are damp and warm, like a baby. Or a fetus! It's like a little part of them is still waiting to be born. It makes me feel stuff. I can't be feeling stuff like that. Not with scissors in my hand, not ever.*

I said all that to some fat, mean ladies who spoke only Spanish.

You liked my blond hair. You always wanted to touch it. *Like feathers*, you said. You made me a rose out of paper and I tore it apart. Everybody said you were a sweet kid. I was a frog, a tadpole, still belching unthinkably in the water.

Aviela and I never played Fuck, Marry, Kill—we played Incarcerate, Deport, Douse with Acid. We kept that game from you because we knew you wouldn't like it. We never asked you to play.

Now Aviela's incarcerated for dousing her girlfriend with acid. She had just turned eighteen, so she was tried as an adult. She was scared the other inmates would kill her in there, so she shaved her head bald and pretends to have cancer. There's no dignity in killing a bitch who's dying already. I go there every month—I've been three times already. Time moves so quickly. Sometimes I have to just lie down still on the kitchen floor and think nothing—they do that in prison sometimes. Just like how I do it, facedown on the floor.

I'm already getting those worry wrinkles you had. You could have just answered me, you know, when I asked you how you got them.

Sometimes when the teakettle screams, I think it's a person.

I was in their apartment when Aviela doused her girlfriend. There was bellowing like a whale who's frantic for a friend. As soon as the acid was thrown, Aviela turned sympathetic and doting. I just stayed where I was until they got in the car and drove to the hospital. I didn't see anything, but in some ways that's worse because now I have to imagine.

I still have Aviela's baby tooth in my pocket. She gave it to me when I lost my first one. She told me it was a replacement. Now I'm thinking of shaving my head, just like her—I'd go to the mall and pretend to be a mannequin. If a man touched my breasts, I would spit lemon juice in his eyes. But would it erode my gums, holding lemon juice in my mouth?

You can see the moving-ness of the world if you concentrate. Everything is always moving, but it doesn't mean anything and it isn't going anywhere. People talk like circles are the only shape that go round and round and never end, but if you follow the outline of any shape, you can go on forever. If it is not self-contained and it does have an end, it is a *line* instead of a *shape*.

So whatever you are, whichever identity your gaseous "spirit" expands to fill, your molecules will perform the same duty, deflecting just as lazily and randomly off the walls.

Don't pity me.

I was lying on my stomach when I realized I didn't want to be a nurse anymore. There was a car crash on the highway last Tuesday. The cars were both red, so they could have been stained with blood and nobody would have known. After I saw the bodies and I was sure none of them was yours, I felt nothing. In the rearview mirror, all I saw was my own reflection in my own sunglasses.

It started to rain. Anyone else would have nudged the person sleeping in the passenger seat. They would have imagined the rain as God's response to the tragedy, never-minding his supposed omnipotence.

My windshield wipers suck, so when it's raining really hard, I can barely see at all. I just keep driving. It's dangerous. I could kill someone. I could blind a little girl in one eye, make her lose all depth perception.

A while ago I started saving up, but then this whole thing happened with Aviela and I quit my job again. It was depressing— people coming in so well-groomed for passport photos. White ladies with dead-fish eyes. Beautiful young women. Tank tops showing bruised-up arms, begging somebody to ask.

I took a photo of a little boy and he said, *That was the only time somebody ever took my picture without bothering me to look happy!* You're not allowed to smile in passport photos—neutral expressions work better for facial-recognition software. The rule is no teeth. I told that to an old man and he took his dentures out.

Some of those people were so ancient, I wondered where they

could possibly be going.

An old, effeminate man wore a turtleneck that came up to his mouth. *I need something to bite down on*, he told me, *for the pain*.

A girl came in crying and her mother whispered to me that she had just *been visited by Aunt Flow for the first time*. I didn't know what that meant.

Two men could not bear to be apart. They asked if I could photograph them together and then crop them into individuals.

A transgender woman found it hard to sit unsmiling. If I knew what to change so I could be that happy, I'd do it too.

She had those high, girlish cheekbones and slanted eyes and silicone boobs. You have to get a new passport picture if you change your appearance so much that the previous picture no longer resembles you.

When my mother got a fake butt, I cried on your shirt, into your young, new breasts, worrying how she wasn't herself anymore. Because if she'd gotten a replacement body part, then she'd been diluted. *But isn't lime water still water?* you said, in that shaking voice, like somebody would come in and see me crying and accuse you of hurting me. *Isn't water still water if you squeeze a little lime into it?*

My hair is as long as I dreamed it would be when I was little. If I do shave it off, I can justly say that *nothing* turned out the way I thought it would—but I'm *only eighteen*, you would remind me. (I now have to play both the part of *me* and the part of *you*.) Even though the width of my kitchen floor hardly accommodates the length of my body, some people would say I'm still a kid. The landlady, for example. Yesterday, she took one of my hands in both of hers and waived the rent for me. She carries birdseed in her pocket, but all the birds have developed a preference for bread.

I'm looking for a new job now. When I quit at the zip line place, my manager tried to get me to stay. I didn't have a long speech this time. All I did was shake my head.

"You're eighteen?"

"Yes."

"Milyada? Is that how you pronounce it?"

I nod. Her eyes look scary, moving fast across the paper. Sometimes I look at people's slightly parted lips and imagine the things I could fit between their teeth.

"You used to live up north?" the woman asks.

"Yes. I did."

"So did I. How'd you like it?"

"Well…" She has a cup of coffee on her desk, polluted with so much cream it looks like chocolate milk. I swallow saliva, pretending it will quench my thirst. "I met a Black lady up there, and she told me how her great-grandparents had come from the South to escape slavery."

She nods, disconcerted. "Yes. It's rich with history. And I do find that, even today, people up north are more tolerant."

"Well, less tolerant of racists."

She smiles, surprised. "Would you consider yourself a racist?"

"No."

"All right, good." She laughs and picks up my résumé again.

"So you wrote—"

"But I think there are lots of racists who wouldn't consider themselves racist."

She pauses. "Yes."

She shuffles the papers. My résumé is too many pages—too many jobs within the span of four years. I watch the woman smile resiliently. I worry about the odor of my body.

"That is true," she reiterates.

Why did you always draw the sun without the shine coming out of it? That bothered me when I was a kid. Everybody else drew lines coming out of the circle, and you left it bald. *That's not even a sun,* I said. *It's just a circle.*

My drawings were characterized by an obsessive too-much-ness. The lines I drew coming out of the sun were many, and extended to the edges of the paper or the beginning of the grass. The grass was not a thick block of green, but instead countless green lines, overlapping hideously. There was not one or two rabbits, but a poorly drawn menagerie, each animal the only one of its species. *What other animal should I draw?* I loved to ask. When no one answered, I asked again, continuing until somebody yelled to stop. When my mother was home, it did not take long.

Why does the sun look white? I asked you when I was small, when people loved me, when I didn't have to braid my own hair and it was soft like puppy fur.

It is white, but don't look at it, because it will hurt your eyes.

But why do we draw it yellow?

Because the paper is white.
Oh.
And because it's easier to look at.
Oh.
Also because… that's just the way everybody draws it.
But it doesn't even look like a circle, Devora!
That's how I remember the conversation. Maybe you remember it a different way. Maybe you remember my hair as less soft. Maybe you know you were smiling not at me but instead at a memory in which I was not involved.

I think about that stuff as I lie on my stomach, trying to think about nothing. It's difficult to think about nothing, because nothing doesn't exist. Even in a hypothetical world where nothing existed, there would be nobody there to think about it.

When I quit my job at the place where I took people's passport photos, I said nothing. I just walked out.

Aviela's girlfriend is sleeping on my couch. It's good to have company. Her face is messed up from the acid (and from before that, the drugs and the fistfights), but she's pretty. Her name is Paige. Aviela knows that Paige is here, and she's okay with it because they already apologized to each other—Paige apologized for kissing her manager and Aviela apologized for dousing Paige with acid.

Paige sleeps with a pillow held over her face like she's suffocating herself. Her feet hang off the edge of the couch, large and flat. If she were smaller, I'm sure Aviela would have just pushed her around instead of dousing her with acid. Paige is over six feet tall.

The first day she moved in, she showed me a picture of a moose on her phone. She didn't say anything, so I just smiled. Later she told me she had been trying to break the ice. I suppose a moose would be good at breaking ice. But does it hurt their heads? To break solid things with their antlers?

Paige doesn't come with me to visit Aviela. They need distance. Neither likes to be within acid-dousing range of the other.

The prisoners with babies make me sad. When they pick the baby up, they hold it out with their arms extended, just looking at it. Looking warily for traces of themselves. Aviela is lucky she's gay.

"Can I see a picture of her?" she asks, impatient, like she has to pee.

"Paige?"

"Yeah. You got one on your phone?"

I show her a video of Paige dancing awfully at Juan's party.

Aviela inhales. "Shit, man."

"What?"

"She's not pretty anymore."

"Well... you know that. You saw her. And *you* doused her with acid."

"She kissed her fucking manager!"

"Yeah."

"She hurt me more than I hurt her," she mumbles, watching the video again. Paige's arms are raised over her head. Her head is down. Her hair moves stiffly, like it has also been hardened by defeat.

"Let's say you hurt each other the same amount," I whisper.

"No, man. No."

Our mother never understood why you took such an interest in us. Twelve-year-old girls think toddlers are cute, but they usually tire easily of them. I wish I remembered the beginning. I wish I knew the first thing you ever said to me. You told me I grabbed your hair. My hands were wet and warm. I wish I could do it now. A handful of long, dark silk.

The first poem I wrote was called "Devora."

I watched you read it, smiling the whole time.

And at the end, you hugged me.

"What did you say to each other?" Paige asks. Her scars are shiny, like decorations. Icicles.

"We just talked."

"Oh," she says. She's eating apricot jelly on white bread. I want her to help me with rent and to pay for some of the food she's eating, but I don't know how to ask her. A study I read says that pretty people have an easier time getting hired, so Aviela might have ruined her chances.

But I think Paige *is* still pretty. The acid didn't burn her lips. Her eyes are still that nice golden brown.

"How do you feel?" I ask.

"I feel good. I actually did something today."

"Oh. What did you do?" The conversation echoes off the cold tile and white walls. Living with Paige, I feel like someone in an arranged marriage between decent white families. We live in an excess of courtesy. There are never any dishes floating in the sink.

"I drew a picture. It's really stupid, though." She holds up the notebook she's been using to chart the progress of her burns. The top of the page says, "REWRAP ARM BANDAGE, 4 ASPIRIN." Below that is a drawing of a girl with the same burns Paige has. Two tears are falling from her eye, but they look more like the tattoos felons get to indicate how many people they have killed. I see where she drew a small circle, a distant sun, above her head. She erased it, though, because some things are better left in darkness.

"I like it," I say.

"Thanks." She holds it close to her. "It's me."

There is a pause because I don't know what to say. The girl in the drawing doesn't look like her. I guess that flat pencil faces never look like anybody you know personally. If I were a criminal, I'd run away so they'd have to get a witness to describe my face and draw it for their posters. That way, I'd know what I look like to strangers.

"Are you mad at Aviela?" I ask.

"Yeah."

"Well, she's mad at you too. That's kind of what we talked about today."

"Yeah. I know. I never meant for it to get like this."

"Me neither."

"You? You weren't really part of it. Don't worry."

I want to tell her that, while it was not my fault, it is certainly affecting my life, but I don't. Her hair smells like organic candy and her scars are scary only when she's mad.

Paige doesn't ask me why I lie on my stomach in the kitchen. I'm scared to bring it up. She steps over me with those redwood legs. Paige doesn't even say, *Aren't you going to get that?* when Miss Landlady starts knocking on the door. I don't know why I ignore the landlady when she's so nice to me. If I opened the door, she would probably be carrying a large plate of chocolate-chip cookies.

I try to put new, unaccustomed skin onto the tile so I can experience again the shock of the cold. Paige turns on the light and spreads jelly. I used to imagine but now I remember.

Aviela ordered the nitric acid online. The bottle cost forty dollars. A week before that, I saw her looking at photos of Indian women with motley, disfigured faces. When I asked her what it was, she adjusted the computer screen so I could see. *Bitch women*, she said.

Looks like dick men, I answered.

Maybe both, she said, and I nodded.

But I didn't agree—I just didn't want to argue.

When our mother befriended yours, we were alone often.

Aviela and I took our dresses off. High vents blew cold air above our heads. You broke dry spaghetti noodles in half to make them easier for us to eat. Our mothers came home with bloody heels, holding hands greedily—like each one was kidnapping the other.

That's what I remember.

I dreamed of being in an orphanage so somebody could pick me from a line of other children. There would be something amazing about me—I'd have wings. *Wow, you have wings. You're so special*, they would tell me. *Like red velvet cupcakes, our favorite.*

You didn't want to play the orphanage game. When you asked to be the orphan, we laughed at you.

I want you to know that now I feel sick when I think of those things. I remember complaining that the spaghetti was too soft. It wouldn't hold its shape. The meal turned to a mush of wheat and tomato sauce. Eating it made me feel like a pig.

Sometimes I think I imagined everything—maybe even you. It would be more logical to assume that it never even existed than to accept that it all somehow vanished.

There was never a time when you could comfortably hold me. I was a little too big and you were a little too small. You tried, but my feet touched the ground and my dress rode up in your arms. Still, I asked you. Every time.

"What would you consider your greatest weakness?"

I pull at the zipper of my jacket. You're not really supposed to wear zippers to job interviews—buttons are considered more professional. Even snaps are better than zippers. "My *greatest* weakness?"

"Yes."

"So my best weakness or my worst weakness?"

"Your..." He pauses, annoyed. Asking a lot of questions is a good thing—I read that. Maybe this is his first time interviewing somebody. "The weakness that is the most weak."

"So the *weakest* weakness."

"Yes."

"Probably stupidity."

"Stupidity? As in a lack of experience?"

"Well... no. Not *comparative* stupidity—just, you know, inherent human stupidity. Like how we do things that benefit us now but destroy us later. Acting on whims. Having emotions."

"Having emotions is your greatest weakness?"

"My weakest weakness." I nod. "Certainly."

Paige licks the jelly off the bread. The landlady is knocking on the door.

"Do you want me to get the door?" Paige asks.

"Don't worry about it."

"I really don't mind, Milyada."

"No, it's okay."

"But... can I?"

"Why? You're lonely?"

She puckers her lips and stares down, disappointed, at her jelly-less bread. I wonder why she bothers with the bread in the first place.

"Fine," I say. "Answer it, but I'm not home."

When she stands up, I move to the couch and lie on my stomach, faint with feeling. My weakest weakness. My face sinks into the cushion so breathing is impossible, and I turn my head sideways. It's better to lie on the floor, because they don't have couches in prison, but I'm too tired to move again.

When the landlady speaks, I almost cry. Her kindness is like a mouthful of jelly—that's why Paige likes her. "Paige!" she says. "How are you?"

"I'm fine, Elyse. How are you?"

"I'm *wonderful*. My daughter is in town, with my grandson. I'm very happy."

"You're a grandmother? You don't look old enough!"

The landlady laughs. I never knew her name was Elyse. "Well... yes... but he's just a baby, and I had my daughter when I was very young. Around Milyada's age."

"Oh."

"Is she here?"

"Milyada? No... No, she's at a job interview."

"Oh, all right. Will you let me know when she's in?"

"Yeah, no problem."

"Thank you. Have a nice day!"

When Paige comes back in, she sits heavily on top of me where I'm lying on the couch. This is the first breach of our overbearing courteousness. For a moment, we're sisters.

"You're stupid," she says.

"I know I am. That's what I told the interviewer today."

"What?" Her weight gets heavier on my back. "You told a potential employer that you were *stupid*?"

"He asked me what my weakest weakness was."

"No wonder you're not landing these jobs! You're supposed to say, like, that you care too much or something."

"But I don't think I care enough."

She touches my hair. "What I was going to say is that you're stupid for not talking to Elyse. She's nice."

"When people are nice to me, I cry."

She gets up. "Whatever."

Immediately, I miss her weight on my back. I consider calling after her, but I can't.

It's true. Remember? The one time you did let us play orphanage, when you pretended to adopt me and you knelt down at the end and stroked my hair and told me that you would love me forever no matter what. Remember? I cried. You made me change my dress because it got dark tear splotches on it. You didn't want our mothers to see.

It was always dark when I washed dishes. I never knew why they couldn't just turn on a light. I never knew why I had to wear a uniform when nobody ever looked at me. They made me wear gloves, but water got inside the gloves and made my hands prune even worse.

I had just gotten back from working at the restaurant the night you left us. As it happened, I was feeling at my pruned hands. Afterward, I thought how ironic it was that my hands were pruned while everything slipped through them. Pruned hands are supposed to be good at holding on to things—that's why it happens. It's an adaption for better grip—because it's so slippery under water, you know.

I thought you had washed your eyes with beet juice, they were so red from crying. I thought you had been making dinner. I thought Aviela had been mashing the beets with her hands. Punching raw beets. Mashed beets? I had never heard of it before. I didn't know you had the energy to think of new dinners for us to try.

What would we have mashed beets with? We need whole grains and we need protein. I would sauté green beans in vinegar. *You like vinegar too much*, you told me. Remember? *The lining of your stomach is going to disintegrate and you'll have no protection against the acid in your blood.*

"You'd be regularly lifting heavy boxes. You can handle that?"

"Yes."

"Good. Good. So can I ask you... why you decided not to pursue higher education?"

"Because," I say, and consider leaving it at that, but continue, "I like lifting heavy boxes."

He tilts his head, one chin doubling and doubling again. "Was that sarcasm?"

"No... I was using the phrase 'lifting heavy boxes' to mean performing menial labor. I don't want to have to think a lot."

He tilts his head again—not downward, but to the side—the layman's way of saying, *Fine. Have it like that.*

"This?" I gesture to the folders and papers. The books. Books about heavy boxes. "It's regurgitation."

He purses his lips and then smiles a sarcastic smile with all his teeth, which look like baby teeth—maybe because his face is so large. "So where do you see yourself in five years?"

"Lifting heavy boxes."

Aviela wants me to sneak her some cocaine. Either cocaine or heroin, she says. A hard drug. She'll give it to the other women so they will like her.

"I think they'll just want more, Aviela," I tell her.

No, she says. They'll be grateful. They'll let her congregate with them beneath the woolen blanket, where they create warmth. They'll whisper memorized poems. It sounds horrible to me, all that cigarette breath. But she wants it so badly.

Both the corners of her mouth are bleeding, like she has been trying to swallow a zebra.

"Is prison food big?" I ask.

"Huh?" She's smiling, nearly banana-colored with happiness.

I feel a parasite in my stomach. "What are you smiling about?"

"Will you bring me the drugs?"

"Tell me why you're happy."

She sighs. "There's a girl named Cecily. Don't you like that name? Isn't it pretty?"

I nod.

"She recites 'Jabberwocky.' All those made-up nonsense words."

I nod. I consider proposing that all words are essentially "made-up nonsense words," but I don't.

"Like *brillig*," Aviela says. "'Twas brillig, and the slithy toves / did gyre and gimble...'"

"Go on."

"I don't know the whole thing. I just think it's pretty cool."

"So you like Cecily?"

"I love her," she says, shaking her head, looking thoughtful. "I want her to know that. So you see why I need the drugs so much."

I nod.

Does love eat away at the enamel of your teeth? Does love fill your stomach with its emptiness? Does love erupt in geysers on your skin? I don't know; maybe it does.

If I put my hair in a bun, I could hide several bags in its hugeness.

"What about Paige?" I ask.

"Yeah, I still love her, okay? Don't tell her about this shit. Tell her I'm doing great. Make it sound real good."

I nod. That's something I've been thinking about a lot—the difference between loving somebody and wanting them to love you.

Nobody told me anything. I was expecting mashed beets, but dinner never came so I boiled hot water and made fennel tea. Our mothers were in prison by then, probably having sex in caged fields, probably grinding pepper with stones and sniffing it to sneeze for that blissful second when they would be forced to close their eyes. Our fathers had never been. You dipped a rag in my hot water, wrung it out, and put it over your swollen eyes.

Aviela is homosexual, you said. *She just told me.*

I know.

You tore the rag from your face. *You know? You knew that?*

Yes.

For how long?

Several years. A while.

No. She's seventeen. How the fuck does she know?

Well, girls are lovely, I said. I reached out and felt the curl of your hair, in front of your ear, my favorite one. *Like this thing. Boys don't have this.*

No. You grabbed my wrist, disgust contorting your face. *Don't look at me. Don't touch me. What? You're sad? You've had a crush on me? It's over.*

That's how I remember the conversation. You might remember it a different way, but if you do, you are wrong. I have not forgotten.

I was fired from my job baking cookies. *Faggot*, he called me.

When I stepped outside, wind blew all the flour from my hair and made me young again. *Fag-got* had a nice rhythm. I thought for a moment about making it my mantra for my morning meditations. *Faggottt*, I said out loud. A construction worker stared up at me from deep in a concrete hole. No, I thought. *T* is a letter with a hard ending. It won't work.

That job was nice. I worked long hours. I rose at 3 a.m. and walked the two miles. It was right after you left. Aviela and I had moved somewhere cheaper—somewhere with roaches and bright red baby roaches. If I had known you were leaving, I would have taken your tooth—a small one that you didn't need. I would have kept it in my mouth, under my tongue. Would it really have been that bad if I had loved you? If it's any consolation, I couldn't and still can't readily describe the difference between platonic and romantic love. It could have been either one. I know only that it hurt.

My cookies were not the best cookies. I was very distracted at the time.

Paige doesn't ask about Aviela. She doesn't comment when I stop buying jelly. She is not unhappy. In her notebook, she has been drawing trees with heart-shaped fruits. She asked me to bring her markers or colored pencils, so I took kids' crayons from a restaurant I interviewed at. Her scars have settled on her face, like sheer curtains covering the skin. If she's fallen in love again, it must be with some inanimate object. She never leaves the apartment.

"Do you love that teacup?" I ask her.

"Huh?"

"Do you love it?"

"Why?" She examines it. "Is it your special cup? I can use a different one."

"You can use any teacup? No preference?"

"Yeah, Milyada. Just let me know. I don't mean to be stepping on your vibe here."

"Do you love the couch?"

"What? It's nice, yeah. What are you getting at?"

"Nothing. Nothing."

Somebody knocks on the door.

I watch her face, slowly understanding. "Do you love the landlady?"

Paige puts a crayon in her mouth, tasting the wax. She's already been poisoned in so many ways. "She's nice, yeah."

*　*　*

I braid my hair so the bun won't come loose. One bag containing six bags with small amounts of cocaine. *How much does it take to get high?* I had to ask the dealer. *Not much*, he told me. *Not much.*

Paige says she likes it—the hairstyle. She asks if I'm going to a job interview. I shake my head—rather violently, to be sure the bag won't fall out. "I'm going to visit Aviela."

"Already? It hasn't been a month."

"It's an emergency."

How will I get the bag out of my hair without appearing suspicious? What if there's a drug-sniffing dog? A drug-sniffing elephant? His one large nostril right upon my head?

I make note of the fact that Paige doesn't ask whether Aviela is okay or not, even when I use the word *emergency*.

Some people who visit their relatives in prison might feel like they are tending to the grave of a loved one.

"Do you have it?" Aviela says, smiling the whole time, her mouth barely moving. Around us, most people are speaking Spanish. Rolling *r*'s like the motor of a boat.

I take my hair out of its bun, slipping the contents discreetly into my fist. Under the table, we hold hands. She puts the bag in her waistband, but I keep her other hand in mine. She gives up trying to pull away, looking suddenly tired.

"Thanks, Milyada," she says. "I owe you."

I smile, waving the comment away.

"Really. What do you want?"

I pause, searching her solemn face for the joke.

"Seriously," she says.

I almost laugh. Money? A mule to carry my things? Things for my mule to carry? A mouthful of triangular teeth that fit perfectly into one another? A colder kitchen floor. One that would numb my whole body and never lose its shocking frigidity. You. Your hair, cool and shiny as a dark, dark river.

"A girlfriend," I say.

Aviela opens her mouth. She smiles. "You're gay? You like girls?"

I nod.

"Man, I thought you were..." She laughs. "I thought you were, like, sexually inept or something. Like, emotionally dead."

I smile. I do it habitually. Sometimes people ask me what I'm smiling about, but they never ask me what I'm frowning about. In high school I wrote a paper on how different animals express emotion. Giraffes use prolonged stares.

"You can have Paige," Aviela says abruptly, leaning back in her chair the way your teachers tell you not to. If her head cracked open, who would mop up the blood? Would the floor be stained a permanent pink? Would Cecily cry? Would Paige?

Once, I was flipping through the channels and I saw a woman stomping around in a bucket full of grapes, about to cry—so strange out of context. Her eyes were watery slits, an ATM of emotion.

Money isn't real, did you know that? It's valuable only because we think that it is.

"Paige is *your* girlfriend," I mutter. I refrain from adding that her face is bleak with scars and that she's so tall she hits her head on door frames.

"One soul can find several mates. Cecily has enlightened me." Aviela smiles. "For example," she whispers, "the Earth is not round."

"What?"

"If it was round, the oceans would be convex. The roads would have a slight curvature. We would see it from the tops of mountains. Is any of that true?" She smiles again. Her tranquility is disconcerting. I wonder if she is already on drugs.

"I've never been to the top of a mountain."

"It's true."

"You've been to the top of a mountain?"

She nods slowly, dizzy with realization. "Remember Devora?"

You enter my mind. You fill the space with rainforest humidity. Animals I thought were extinct show themselves finally. A snake curls in circles, considering the paradox of eating itself.

"Of course I remember her," I whisper.

"She took me up to Mt. Coolidge after I told her I was gay. That morning, when you were at school. We talked about it. The gay thing. She said she had been noticing the way you looked at her."

I blink, dazed and hollow-boned.

"I told her she was crazy," Aviela adds.

"You know," I start slowly, "she was right. I never even thought about being gay. I just knew that I loved her. But when you told me you were gay, I knew that I was too."

Aviela nods, serene. "I always thought that the Earth was round. That vast, flat earth right before my eyes. And to think... all this time, I could have seen... but I never did until Cecily showed me."

*   *   *

Paige is going out to celebrate the landlady's birthday. I was not invited. She curls her hair and wears a shirt that shows her collarbones. I hate collarbones; they make a person look emaciated.

"Paige?"

"Uh-huh."

"How old is she turning?"

"Um... why?"

I shrug. Why are Paige's arms so long, and why, with those long arms, could she not have deflected that acid from her beautiful face? Why can't I imagine Cecily as anything other than a figment of Aviela's imagination? Why does the ocean not curve, and why do boats not move slowly uphill?

"Forty-seven," Paige says.

"That's not too old," I say.

She smiles. I wish you could see her smile. I'm glad we're not giraffes—I'm glad we're human.

"You've had twelve jobs since you were fourteen. You're eighteen now, aren't you? Three jobs a year? Tell me about that."

"Well... I'm ready to settle down now."

"Whoa, whoa! We're not getting married!" The woman laughs. She chokes on a sip of water. "It's not a test, honey. We've always had high turnover here. It's fine! I'm just curious."

"I was looking for something, but it wasn't in those places."

"Do you think you'll find it here?"

"Well... I thought that the Earth was round, but it doesn't look round to me anymore, and just in case it isn't, I don't want to go too far. I don't want to move around anymore. Your body can't decompose in space. It freezes."

She nods.

"I knew what I wanted, but I didn't want myself to have it, because I was afraid. It's like hungry people drinking water with spoons. Eating cotton balls, throwing up, wondering why their fingers taste salty. Salty with what? You know?"

She doesn't reply.

"It's not that I had a reason to leave—I just didn't have a reason to stay. Everywhere I go, I look for a reason to stay and I find nothing."

Her presence suddenly offends me, like she is a black hole and I am simple matter being pulled. I resent her for listening to the things I am telling her. Who knows what she's hiding in her hair?

"Okay? I don't know! That's what I'm looking for. You know how many interviews I've been to? People asking me about myself? I don't know about myself! I sit there and just *speculate* about what kind of a person I might be. You should be telling me. Well? Who am I? What am I like?"

You didn't leave anything. Not a tooth, nothing. Now you're probably having sex with a man, making out in a poppy field, shopping for seasonal attire, things with buttons instead of zippers, asking young women what their greatest weakness is, riding zebras when they're not meant to be ridden, showing the barber a photograph of Taylor Swift, smiling obtusely for a passport picture, crying and shaking on zip lines, smiling at a man, figuring out a comfortable way to hold such a huge hand, having little to no knowledge of the emotional lives of giraffes, boiling your own water, eating only half the meal somebody served you, telling people about your incarcerated mother and those sick, strange children you brought up as your own. Maybe you have heard of Aviela, a felon. Your worried wrinkles may have deepened, but I'm sure if I looked at you, I would still love you. I would understand how Aviela could come so close to killing and still claim that her own pain was greater than her victim's. I would feel sorry for Paige. For myself. Acid wouldn't hurt so much if it were thrown by someone who'd never loved you.

THE ISLAND

by GABRIELA JAUREGUI

WE RISE FROM OUR slumber. We lick the tips of our fangs. In the heart of the city's center, in the navel of this belly that was once a metropolis and is now a cake ruin—layers and layers of the detritus of civilizations and uncivilized humans; of warriors and those defeated by life; of women of the night; of the ruins of Great Temples and lesser ones, like La Peninsular, El 33, Guagüis, El Internet, Perverts' Lounge, Marrakech; of lone cowboy boots and time-frayed polyester shirts; of headdresses made from the feathers of the formerly extinct quetzal; of tezontle; of the flowers of huauzontle; of asphalt, of corn, of axolotl and anklets and beads of gold and tin; of old books by new authors and new books by old authors; of rubber stamps and empty Tetra Paks of a drink called Boing!; of dentures made with human teeth; of knives with teeth; of 100 percent cotton socks and flat soccer balls; of hanging sneakers; of tiger-striped jockstraps, jaguar pelts, and giant speakers that now serve as our homes; of flower water and alarm clocks with their *tee-teeteetee teeteeteetee*s forever silent—we awaken.

Our burrow is in this underground system of tunnels, whose entrance is found under Dos Naciones, a former lesser Temple that is nothing but rubble now save for its door. In this tunnel under the street once called Simón Bolívar, named for a hero from their history, which is not ours, at the break of day, at the crack of dawn, no one breaks or cracks us. Not anymore. We are mistresses of these streets. Of all streets and places, of all doorways, entrances, and portals. Of these 669 blocks of ruins. They all belong to us. Here, we are alpha bitches. Beyond, there are others. But here in this land that is yours and everyone's, little pup, you'll live and learn to walk. Learn to swim in this cake island at the center of five lagoons. But first, listen to this tongue that licks your ear, that licks your eyes, to this mother tongue telling you: *Listen to your story, the one I sing.* Here is your fang-severed umbilical cord. I'm from here, you're from here, from here we will be.

We rise from our slumber. In the heart of the city's center, in the navel of this belly that was once a metropolis, you are born. From this belly of mine that was all yours I give birth to you in spring. You've arrived on this earth to sing to the moon. To converse with dusk and with dawn. I sing to you in this tongue as I lick you. I bring you into being, little one, with our mother tongue. Now we awaken but first we had to emerge from a nightmare. Their nightmare. They destroyed tigers and eagles. With their black ink, they erased brotherhood, community, nobleness. You can hear these laments, these songs, these recordings from the past in magnetic tapes, in shiny CDs, in these notebooks and obsolete formats the ghost voices sing. But seven centuries on this earth did not keep our howl from rising to the top of the Torre Latinoamericana, now nothing more than a bent spine. Though it be jade, it cracks; though it be gold, it breaks; though it be "Made in China" plastic, it splits, as the ancients used to say. But this bone and fur, they last. Our teeth have torn and will tear yet. Our wild fangs were here only for a while, but that while got a little longer, then longer still. It started with "Life's a bitch," then moved on to bitches getting down and perreo. Humans imitating us. They always wanted to be like us. Crazy monkeys. But they never had the courage or the nose to see it through. Listen here, coyotita: they withered on their own, they yellowed. This time we beat them. Bitches, coyotas, gray wolves, all of us. We came back. And so, four by four, like a flower, they dried up here on earth. We flourished. Like cacti, like succulents, we bloomed. We managed our thirst until the center, the navel, the heart filled up again—with blood, then water. With licking pleasure we drank the blood first. Bitches, coyotas, gray wolves. With this tongue, you hear. That scar left from our life inside the belly—the navel—fills with water when we lie faceup under the rain, and so this basin filled up again and that's how we flourished. Swimming doggy-style. The others went to the place of the fleshless, and we stayed here.

We rise from our slumber, my pup. Our litters born in burrows in churches, in pawnshops, under painted murals. We emerged from our slumber when the cages of those little birds opened, those birds that had been our neighbors on the streets, in the hallways, on dusty patios, under roofs of loud tin—when those birds born to extract tiny fortunes printed on colored paper and who died as amulets for human love—flew. They were all flying, flying. The most fortunate bird, the one who pulled fortunes for the women intoxicated in front of a bridal shop window, was the one who announced the lake of blood. From the doorsteps where we'd get kicked in the mornings, we heard her—in the projects and markets and Frikiplazas, we rang in her song, its portent: all that is true, all that has roots, shall prevail here.

Slumber no more. Listen well, xocoyotita, to the song of the early risers. We eat what is true. Here in the center, inside the heart, we make our own words and leave our traces, pawprints in the mud. Friends, eagles, jaguars, butterflies, foxes, cyborgs, night crawlers, otters, chicken hawks, hawkers, vendors, and poets—they all went to the place of mystery after drinking from the flowers that intoxicate, the flowers of the rainy season and open corollas. There, the bird jabbered and sang of the place of mystery. We knew how to listen. With our howls and the birdsong, we rejoiced. Our howling was heard in the distance, up high near the tips of television antennas at the northernmost edge. From Alameda to Lagunilla, we rejoiced; from Merced to Mixcalco markets we rejoiced; all the way to the Arena México, there we were, licking our lips. This whole island is our territory. This land of waste we inhabit. Our land of cake and lake, the detritus of history on which we leave our mark, make our home.

Experience taught us about heels and pointed shoes, about the choke collar; we knew of abuse, of sticks, of tight ropes and pulled chains. Experience taught us about loneliness, hunger; about hands holding dry tortillas and the hands of girls, soft petals of the flower that intoxicates. Experience taught us about leftover snout-and-tripe tacos from Los Cocuyos, the empty shells of river shrimp outside the Danubio: we knew all this and more. We sniffed shit and vomit; we sniffed bellies and guitars in Garibaldi, mezcal spilled like an offering to the ancients, rancid pulque, the scent of gardenia. Experience taught us about transparent platform shoes. We licked those feet, we knew the precious anklets. We knew the marches of humans who were as hopeless as we were back then. We shared the warm volcanic zócalo floor and cold doorsteps with them. We knew the swift hum of the subway, that unplumed orange serpent snaking through the entrails of this center, in the place of heat and darkness, until it slowed to a stop, braked, broke. We sniffed pits, we sniffed tzompantlis and wooden rosaries. We watched sinkholes swallow homes and sniffed the heavy dust that rose from the holes. We hid. We slept on the doorstep of history, their human history. The ones who offered themselves up were abandoned, mistreated. They left for the place of the fleshless. Good news for us, bad omen for them. We ate meat. Lots of meat. We survived, we endured here on this earth. Then friends came and invited us to pleasure, we were intoxicated together, we bonded, we fucked, we left. We fled. We flew. We became many, multiplied like froth in cacao. We became a pack. Standing among corn and bones, we left. We were born abandoned, so no one orphaned us. We were never separated by a cage. Singers, birds, motley canines: let it be so, let us raise our song, my little one.

Time to rise here. Listen here. May your heart open, bring your heart close. Take your teat. Do not seek my death, cub. One day soon enough I will leave for another house, a different doorstep.

Doorsteps and door frames remained in the shape of arches, like candles on this cake of ruins, without houses behind them, without housing projects to be entered, without stores, bodegas, bars, or restaurants. Nothing more than mere appearance. Thresholds, the essence of the doorstep, our good place on this earth. It is here that we are masters of the close and the together, of the near and dear, of pleasure. They tried to erase us, but it was they who withered. Now we live in the place of their loss. Close and together. Without the statues of horses. Without their DVD- and CD-cloning machines, without their Holy Death, their Saint Jude, without their Virgins, Kings, Viceroys. This is how we begin to find ourselves; we are coming together. Where shall we go? We will go to rip and tear, my littlest one, my socoyota. Like breath, we rise. We sprout like tender green corn. This is how you burgeon forth from the belly, in the navel of what was once called New Spain, or DF, or CDMX, or Anáhuac, also known as the bowl of cream, or the great Tenochtitlán.

And suddenly we rose from our slumber like grass in spring. Open your eyes, pup. We will delight in our song. Feel the cold tip of my wet snout nudging you. Get up, come on. Go, make this giant ruin yours. Piss on it. Make its dust mud with your urine, deck the vestiges of older times with your shit. Here in this time, we share the gifts, food, what gives shelter, doorsteps for all, the land, water, flower, corn, and meat to be ripped. Hear the voices of your pack calling to you. Urging you on. Come, run. Our howls rain down like emeralds and egret feathers. This is how we speak. With perfumes and flowers, we speak. Feel our pack in your heart. Feel the rhythm of our paws with each beat. Feel your belonging. Become us. Everywhere is your home. Every doorstep in the center. This is our territory, yours now, little heart newly sprouted. Inhabit it. Draw a line from Mina to República del Perú, Apartado, Leona Vicario, República de Guatemala, Avenida del Trabajo, Arcos de Belén, and Eje Central, then all the way to Avenida Juárez. Trace the outline of this island in your heart, then paint these streets with your piss, with your florid song. Not in vain are we here on this earth, this land, our flowery patio. Not in vain did we fight to endure in this place of the fleeting moment.

Now we awaken and you answer your pack with a howl, and so we rejoice. In the center of this land, everywhere, is your home. Here, where the many flowery trees stand and where there are no more war drums, and no more metal weapons, and no more chains. Here in this navel: sing, howl, answer your pack with your newly emerged teeth. With your teeth like bloody needles, at dawn you will emerge from the burrow. It's your turn now, young one. Go out and hunt with your tiny, sharp teeth. Tear apart what remains of them. Let them be drenched in blood, those who tried to erase us. Separate us. Let us go to their ruins, to their crooked, fallen buildings. Let us go to their cages. To their useless factories. To where they yellowed and withered. In their ruins you will find them. Bite their heels. When they fall, eat their faces; eat their eyes, jocoyotina; adorn yourself with their necklaces and sharpen your tiny teeth on their ribs until the jacaranda flowers rain down upon you in spring. And we will howl with you.

CHIMBOTE HIGHWAY

by JULIA WONG KCOMT
translated by JENNIFER SHYUE

THOUSANDS OF KILOMETERS GO by before my disquiet starts to fade. There's a strong smell. Between daydreams and carsickness, the big sign announcing the city's name comes into view. The highway is a strip of intestine that shows no mercy to nausea, that demands to be displayed in its idiosyncrasy despite its incomprehensible length; it makes us wonder why it's named the Pan-American. Does it occupy all of the Americas, crisscross them, envelop them; is it so long that colloquially we'd say it's impossible to make heads or tails of it? It widens in just a few places; mostly it's narrow, neglected, dried-up, closed in on both sides by stretches of desert where mirages in the distance mimic water. The only thing that rises up, again, modest and unforgettable, is the old green sign framed in white that repeats: CHIMBOTE.

They always give us kids these awful pink plastic bags because they know that at some point we'll throw up. They buy them in bulk. It's as if the blankness of those spaces compels our weak little stomachs to empty out. We can't keep anything in, everything tosses and turns. But we're relieved when it's over. Throwing up is annoying, but it's also soothing.

The boredom of the adults in the car is obvious. They are easily infected. Us, not so much. My brother, my cousins, and I are constantly alert to what's happening. The changes. I've been counting the poles and the red escarabajos. (These are the VWs they call "vochos" in Mexico and "Beetles" in English-speaking countries. Honestly, I don't see how they look at all like ladybugs or like any bug, but that's another thing about city folks: we associate objects with animals by their shape. The worst is when there are no shapes to make associations with, just the emptiness left by the people who used to be there.)

I've counted 345 poles since we left Chepén but only three red Beetles. I'm getting a little bored; we've been driving down this stretch for a while, sentenced by the sand that weaves from one side of the highway to the other. Until a few years ago, when I was still a kid (when I was really little), I never got bored, I counted the poles without ever missing one, watchful, always watchful, I admired the hills, I loved the colors of the sand, especially as they changed in the dimming light. On the stretches where you could make out the sea, I'd be about ready to burst with excitement—the car was carrying us away from Chepén.

I've long hated Chepén, its thirst, its backwardness, its lack of interest in being anything more than a poor region flavored with drifting sand and grotesque apparitions. But shriveled as it was, it was a landscape of our own, like the scene of a lunar disaster. Fields sown with rice and legumes dominate the valley's landscape now, but my gaze and my feelings were focused on the desert that made its presence felt beyond the fertile plots. Lots of people here believe in using witchcraft to do harm to others. There are all sorts of contraptions and objects they can use to hurt or *trabar* someone, from desiccated animals to chunks of perfumed wood.

We were raised as Chinese children, not Peruvian children. Our furniture was all wicker and our dishes were blue-and-white china. In the morning we ate with forks and at night we ate with chopsticks, or *fai chi*. Our spoons were always glass or porcelain, depending on the occasion. We'd break lots of them during the year, in accidents or because they were fragile. My parents were in charge of replacing them. There was a box in the kitchen full of Chinese spoons.

Chinese children wash their faces with towels that have been dipped in boiling water. When we're small, the adults scrub behind our ears with them. Papá would do it: first T.K., then me; my mother didn't like to touch us.

Tedium has settled in Chepén: the accidental tourist and the medical representatives are oblivious to the enigmas that surround us. There were tons of pharmacies in Chepén. Most of the medical representatives were tall, well-dressed, and pale-skinned; they looked like models from an ad. They sold regulated medications produced in laboratories in Switzerland or the United States. In the '70s, the decade when I discovered and was left awestruck by the medical representatives, medication wasn't produced in Peru; it was mostly imported. I couldn't help but associate the medical representatives with elegance, good health, and foreign countries. But we lived alongside traditional knowledge: the women who made *amarres* so men would stay at their side, fuck them well, or "tend" to them; the shamans who presided over burials of clothing and knit dolls, invoking ill wishes, sickness, and dark omens. I grew up seeing two kinds of signs: the ones for curanderos, who dispensed strange infusions with Indigenous names, and the ones for evangelical churches offering salvation. For me, the pharmacies were gleaming hospitals where medical representatives would visit with their perfect leather suitcases to offer health via pills and neat little syrups. Chepén was a small vessel for foreign energies, with two pharmacies on each of its four streets. I always wondered why there were two pharmacies on every street.

I also wondered why there was so much medication on offer. Were we that sick? Why did people consult them all: the herbalist, the curandero, and the doctor? I don't know if ours was a town of sick people, but it seemed like we were all missing something, were irritated, aching, unwell. Why? Where did all that discomfort come from? Could it be the desert and its dryness? Had we been dropped into some kind of hell? Sometimes I'd look at the city's surroundings and it would dawn on me that we lived among trash. Was that the reason? What curse had expelled us from some verdant place and left us there, where donkeys shit on the cobblestone streets and deeply hewn shortcuts, where dogs looked like moribund pessimists and signs offered herbs and spells?

Perhaps its early inhabitants were the ones who established a tradition according to which healing and health amid the sand required constant reinforcement. They understood that our lives were in danger in a place founded upon inhospitality, precarity.

There are several minor Catholic saints with a diverse range of features: African, Indigenous, Spanish, Italian. Their engravings hang in many of the houses. The faces of those martyrs, their puffy eyes with humongous dark circles, would fill me with an indescribable terror. They seemed more sickly than their devout. I didn't think we should be praying to them, because if they couldn't even take care of their own health, they certainly couldn't protect ours. Almost all of us kids experienced a *limpia*, almost all of us were cleansed with an egg, or a cuy, or wads of spit produced by horrible, gaunt witch doctors. But of all the cousins, I was the one they bathed most often with strange herbs and draped with amulets against evil. "It's because you're not baptized," my mother would say like it was a secret, unrepentant but knowing that was why the "evil eye" could fall doubly on me.

In addition to these rituals, we children of Chinese families would be given remedies brought from China, *po chai pills* (tiny, round maroon pills useful for all sorts of things), concoctions made with kión (ginger), and, most of all, a shift in diet: lots of vegetables, fish, slow-cooked soups with fungi extracted from tree bark. The kitchens of Chinese immigrants looked like enormous pharmacies, full of bottles and containers with seeds and indescribable condiments. There were also eggs left to "spoil" in salt, spicy fermented tofu, fish salted and preserved until worms came out, dried duck, and other foods processed according to thousand-year-old recipes.

I was always bewitched by the silvery sea as we left Trujillo. At the edge of every city along the coast, the Pan-American spreads out, majestic, as if emerging from its hideaway. It comes into view where the metropolis abandons its vanity, surrounding the city, suffocating it, cutting through it at unexpected angles. The stretches where it expands, straight and pretentious, offer lessons in superiority:

without the Pan-American, these places would be isolated from one another. The highway is a long asphalt snake uniting the continent longitudinally. Without it, no one would know what lies beyond the valleys, or whether the America in its name has breadth and width or is just an invented thing.

I shiver when I catch my first glimpses of the Pacific illuminated by strong, indiscreet rays of sunlight. Those dry hills must be inhabited by foxes, animals full of tales and knowledge of how to run from heat or bullets. Some die crossing the highway, unaware that the cars are faster than they are nimble. They use their beige pelts as natural camouflage against the desert's aggressions. I always liked those imposing landscapes the most.

The image that returns again and again to my memory is of a girl with a big head, left to her fate for spending so much time in reverie, aimless and with no self-control; she presses her nose against the window of her uncle's car and stares out at the desert. The car moves south, the first emptiness is just outside of San Pedro de Lloc. Something magical happens when I watch the light's distortions as it refracts across that vast layer of sand and dunes peppered with weeds and the birds of prey they call vultures.

My recollection of this stretch of desert starts in Pacasmayo and ends when we arrive in Chimbote. A few strange pines, the outlandish stench of foxes obliging us to smell the farts they mark their territory with, which could've been labeled "derived from fish meal." Some clueless people think it's the smell of anchovies being processed. Whether it's from fox farts or dried anchovies, this city in the north has its own enigmatic smell: Chimbote begins and ends in its own essence.

The desert has a nobility to it, and the simple things, the color of the sand, are clear, clean. But there are also hidden parts, where the foxes do their thing and are accomplices to that mystery from which we men, women, and children are far removed. Where there's no room for God, or San Sebastián—the gay saint of Chepén—or the Virgin of Guadalupe, much less the saints from the capital, no matter how dark-skinned or flagellated. There's room only for embattled foxes; it's as if there were invisible foxes watching over Chimbote, clamoring for justice.

In some stretches, the water rebels along its invisible course, and there the desert greens. Modest fields appear and the steel blue sea forcefully cools the coast. This makes the sands look seductive, luxurious in a way that mimics dark, monarchical traditions of beauty. Cleopatra. The Queen of Sheba. In Peru there are no empires in the desert; the desert is an empire.

Some Moche lineages won battles. Of those I have no word, I know only about the terrible marks they left on their prisoners of war.

Maybe my mother, by cleaning the living room three or four times a day, was facing off against the sand as a key element of everything that surrounded us. It was a struggle to control its movements and its capricious way of spreading across surfaces, covering everything over. But the sand rules alone. On the other hand, the best kingdoms are the ones where you can't feel the king. At home, we've capitulated to the power of the sand that sneaks in everywhere. We don't even say to ourselves that at least we're less dirty than people in other places. It is what it is. It's all we know.

The desert is elegant, made of sand and wind, and the sand is omnipresent in our lives, on the horizon, in the cupboards, the shoes, the houses, the bathrooms. Sometimes it even lands on the food, as if to remind us that we can't escape it.

I was born in the middle of this desert dampened by warped rivers, this place where the waters refused to be contained. A rocky desert, undignified. Skittish. Where men and women seemed to pair up only to reproduce, since the word *love* had no place in this landscape. Only the Jequetepeque Valley saves us from starving and shriveling. I was born in the middle of the sand and the wind, on a day when mothers regret having uteruses and placentas. I was born in a place that sometimes feels like part of the shattered humidity, as if the sporadic rains were consolation for their very irony, but Chepén is too close to the sand. It's as if the gravity exerted by the hill burst the bubbles we allowed ourselves to form with this sparse moisture. I grew up running my index finger over the furniture, and I know how stubborn and erratic dirt and sand can be: as soon as you clean a surface, new grains appear. Chepén was founded on the slope of this squat mountain. Its history is that of four streets and a train that transported sugarcane. Many Chinese people came to the sugar and rice plantations, among them my papá. It used to be a town where a whistle sounded every day at two thirty in the afternoon to announce that everyone's vegetable soup was about to be dusted with the ashes of burned sugarcane. Now it's a city that has learned to negotiate with the capricious rivers that encircle it. Instead of sugarcane they sow rice, corn, even rosebushes and mountain grasses. But whatever the desert swallows is incorporated, as if through magic, into its beauty, so much so that it no longer has a name. It just disappears.

A VOLCANO
IS BORN

by Brenda Lozano
translated by Heather Cleary

IT IS TOLD THIS WAY:

NOT SO LONG AGO, on a winter's afternoon in a small town in Mexico, a volcano was born. As the youngest volcano in the world, it is the only one with an ample record of the years following its birth beside the home of Demetrio and Bernarda.

Demetrio, who owned the tract of land where the volcano was born, was plowing the soil with two oxen one afternoon when he heard a rumbling underground. He thought it was an earthquake like the one that had shaken the town days earlier, raising clouds of dust and covering his roof boards with dirt. The rumbling was followed by a slight tremor that raised only a thin puff of dust, like the ones that formed and vanished as the oxen walked. Other weak tremors, sensed by a few of the animals, followed one another like a line vanishing into the horizon. Demetrio was plowing his land and thinking about how he would need to sweep the dirt from his roof boards again when suddenly he heard an explosion like a sharp crack underground. His oxen spooked and a wisp of smoke began to rise from the earth.

Demetrio hurried back to the house to tell Bernarda what had just happened; she left in search of the priest to tell him what was happening on their land. In those days, the priest was supervising the construction of a church that would bring the two neighboring towns together. The priest was not at the unfinished church, but one of the builders told Bernarda to look for him at his troje. Demetrio paced, not knowing what to do, as the sun set and a wisp of smoke continued to rise from behind his home. The smoke seemed endless, like how night follows day. That wisp of smoke reminded him of the tornado that had once formed on the other side of the milpa when he was a boy; it had come upon him at a sprint as the dogs barked, and if he remembers anything, it is that feeling of terror and the roar of the raging air when it twists itself into a tornado.

Bernarda returned to their land with the priest just before night fell, and the three of them examined by candlelight the place where the wisp of smoke had risen but no longer rose, as if it were hiding underground. There was nothing but a long, long crack in the ground, like the ones that open during a drought before the first rains of spring. There was no smoke, but the earth was as hot as a comal over a flame. The priest could not fathom why the earth was so hot, how its temperature could have changed, or why it smelled so strange. When he smelled the odor coming from it, so fetid it was as if the earth were dying inside, he closed his eyes and began to pray. Bernarda followed suit, while Demetrio, his mind completely blank, simply closed his eyes.

Demetrio couldn't sleep that night. What would happen if the earth thundered again? What if the smoke was a terrible omen? What if God was punishing them? And what would happen if the wisp of smoke became a tornado? A tornado incubating down there that—as soon as it touched the earth, like a colt fresh from the mare—would take his crop and the milpa with it. What would happen if that wisp of hot smoke with its violent smell killed his oxen and goats? His wife slept like a rock despite the day's strangeness. Demetrio drank one cup of water after another that night, as if unsure what to do with his wakeful body. He finally managed to doze off, and the little sleep he did get mingled with sounds that came either from his dreams or from the depths of the earth, he did not know which. Just before the sky began to lighten, at that hour when the sun's first rays faintly announce their presence and the horizon seems to have caught fire, he opened the door to his home and saw a small black hill that had not been on his land a few hours before. But what was a small black hill doing on his doorstep? How had it gotten there? No one in town could have possibly done them the wrong of putting a small black hill on their land. Demetrio walked toward the newborn volcano, which at that hour of the morning looked darker than the night, and the sun's first rays seemed to want to hold it out to him with open hands. There it was: a black hill the size of a parish church. With a strange hole at its peak.

The hole at the peak of the newborn volcano changed shape right in front of him, as if it were a living thing. Demetrio stared at it. It looked like one of the horseshoes they have so many of on the haciendas. It was changing shape, but he thought it looked like the muzzle of a newborn animal that had come with its unknown language from the depths of the earth. When day broke, the newborn volcano grew a bit more, and when the sun came out from between the mountains, Demetrio could no longer see his neighbor's milpa, and a vast guilt swelled in him.

None of the houses or trojes in town had more than two rooms; most houses had only one and were built of adobe slabs that held the heat in during the winter and stayed cool in the summer. Some had wooden walls that let in the sun's rays in the morning to form strips of light and shadow on the dirt floors; others had their kitchens outside in a little hutch; some had no roof; several had chicken coops and pigs and other animals in pens; and there were a few pine-beamed trojes that had been passed down from generation to generation. Some of those had been around for two or three centuries, which made the town look like something from another time. The priest's troje and his tract of land had been gifts from one of the landowners in the next town over, in exchange for officiating at the first communion of his twin daughters on his avocado plantation.

The church—a pile of stones, dirt, lime, concrete, and three pillars that were about as useful as three legs on a table—had a courtyard paved with concrete where a market was set up every weekend. There was no high school in town, or in the next town over, and no one knew or wanted to know what high school was for, but there were three pulquerías where you could buy aguardiente, rum, and tequila. One of them was famous for the spicy mix of roasted peanuts, fava beans, and corn they made fresh every day. There were no hospitals around, and the nearest clinic—a dilapidated structure with blown-out fluorescent bulbs—was miles away, but there was an older woman with heavy breasts who was no more than four and a half feet tall and wore her hair in the same braids crossed over her back as she had in her adolescence. She tended to the ill and the lovesick with her herbs and her mushrooms and the fire circles she made in little tins to perform her rituals—she always made the same circles on her land, creating different geometries inside them that she translated according to her visitor's affliction, as if the affliction itself were speaking to her, dictating the patterns. If she lit one of her fire circles at night, by morning the rumors were already swirling about what deal she'd made with the devil. It was also known that she was the only person in any of the surrounding towns who could take unwanted children from the sight of God; she would make an elixir in those same empty tins she used for her fire circles and she would give it to pregnant woman who did not want to give birth. They came to see her from far away; she was a woman of few words with no husband or children. Not much was known about her past, but everyone knew that when she was a little girl, her father had been gunned down for casting spells and that she had watched him die.

The townspeople gathered for Mass every Sunday in the court-yard of the unfinished church. There was a canopy held up by five log posts, the tallest one at the center, and from it hung strings of white paper flowers that the wife of the avocado plantation owner had commissioned for the first communion of their twin daughters as a gift to the town, since the party had been on their hacienda. This was the only elegant detail in the entire town, like a delicate brooch pinned on a coarse garment. The nearest cemetery, which was next to a forest, was shared with the neighboring town. One night each year, on the Day of the Dead, most of the townspeople walked by candlelight along the edge of the forest that divided the two towns, sipping corn atole that they heated in great copper pots to ward off the cold. Families shared food to pass the night, and Demetrio and Bernarda usually joined one of them. Their children lived four hours away, except the eldest, who had settled in the United States without papers after crossing the desert on foot with other men from their town. Demetrio and Bernarda often spent the Day of the Dead with a family whose son had also crossed the desert on foot; they would bring offerings for their youngest daughter, who had died in a tragic accident caused by the mud that formed along the banks of the river during the summer rains.

Demetrio and Bernarda's tract of land, like those of almost everyone in town, was vast. Each house was a long walk from the next, except the small ones built on the town's lone avenue—which, scrawny, dusty, and neglected, was like a stray dog everyone knew. The hectares between Demetrio's house and his neighbor's seemed to have shrunk with the birth of the volcano, which grew and grew, slowly blocking out the horizon. Its stench was growing stronger and more unpleasant, like a dead animal drawing flies, but it was also unlike the sweet odor given off by animals that die under the sun's rays. Demetrio thought he might be able to pour lime into the mouth of the newborn volcano to cover the stench, at least, to over-power it with the help of his oxen and a few men; he was thinking that there was no reason for the earth to be so violent, being made by the hands of God, and that maybe he could destroy the newborn volcano, when it grew a bit more right in front of him, right under his nose.

That was the night of the exodus. A landowner who had contracted an agricultural engineer to plan his vegetable garden came over from the neighboring town, which was how the soldiers and the two geologists arrived. That was the night of the exodus, and when Demetrio and Bernarda looked back they saw the first spurt of lava set their home ablaze. In the distance, they could see how the burning rock flowed slowly from the peak, how it illuminated the neighbors' milpas in its descent, how in its slow descent it set fire to all it touched. The roofing caught right away, the trojes swelled with flames. How could the land be so violent? The thick lava—black and orange, such serene colors, so harmonious—destroyed everything in its path with its blaze; Demetrio thought he saw the cemetery that held the body of the little girl they would visit on the Day of the Dead catch fire, and after that he decided not to look back again.

Five nights and six days after the exodus, the newborn volcano had grown to three times its original size, bigger than any cathedral anywhere in the faith, and the residents of the two neighboring towns settled in a campsite on land the soldiers designated while the government decided where to relocate them. They numbered 2,839 and one baby, who, with Bernarda's help, had been born before dawn on the first day of the exodus. At the end of those nights and days, in the distance, they could see the volcano's full shape and one church pillar, the only thing its birth had left intact.

The priest recited prayers with small groups of townspeople. He spoke to them of the miracle of God, of Jesus, who walks beside them, of the Holy Ghost. Nonetheless, the first thing the volcano had destroyed when it was born—aside from Demetrio and Bernarda's land, which had happened almost by chance, because it could have been born in any other town, anywhere in the world, or, for that matter, in any other age, but the volcano seemed to have made a decision, as it if had had an agenda or, rather, an obsession— the first thing the volcano had destroyed was the faith of many, and many poured their faith into work or the money that came with the tourists who flocked to the area.

IT IS ALSO TOLD THIS WAY:

The rumor spread quickly that the devil was getting ready to emerge through the crack in the earth that had just opened on our land. Before it came, I didn't understand that a volcano could show up on your doorstep the way drunks sometimes do in the morning hours. Demetrio went off with the other men who were milling around with their eyes on the black hill that had burst through the ground, they even tasted the earth from that ridge, with its smell like the dead. There were a few quakes before it began to peek through, but we had grown accustomed to them because they were soft, like two people telling secrets so no one else can hear. Afterward, we cleaned our rooftops with brooms, but those quakes were just the earth sneezing, we never imagined that a dead hill would push its way through the crack. I barely felt the last one, the one that birthed the volcano. I thought: Bernarda, it's an earthquake. I didn't think: It's an earthquake that will bring with it a hill that smells like the dead. But it did: it wasn't just a little quake, it brought the volcano we thought was a dead hill with a hole at the top, the volcano we believed was there because the devil wanted to punish us all. But nothing came out of that soft spot on its newborn skull, all it did was move. I thought: Nothing's going to come out of that hole, that hill is probably just useless. Sometimes useless children are born into hardworking families, and maybe that ridge with its smell like the dead is useless like them, not even good for burning trash, out there among the others that are good for raising crops.

There was Demetrio with the other men, staring at it. We already knew we had to leave, because a gentleman told the soldiers that the thing on our doorstep was a volcano, that it wasn't the devil. I went into our home and gathered our packs and I waited for Demetrio to tell me we were leaving, because I don't give the orders around here. And he said to me: Bernarda, let's go. So we went. We left the ridge and its smell of death behind on our land. The smell was everywhere and it frightened us all.

Demetrio carried the packs and I brought the goats and the oxen. I couldn't carry the packs because all the little ones I've brought to the town had ruined my back. We gathered in the church courtyard, the Father spoke to us of Exodus from the Bible, he told us that God our Lord had a new place in store for us and we set off walking with our packs, trunks, and plow teams, with our mules, goats, hens, and pigs, with our food gourds, our crates, pots, and chairs, and even with our decorations. The newly born volcano gave off its first lava that night. From the camp we could see its blaze and red glow. Demetrio was frightened, I know the face of stone he makes when fear is trapped inside him, but I wasn't frightened, because it looked pretty from far away and because I thought: Bernarda, this is God's will. Someone said to me that the earth had felt smothered and just needed a place to breathe. I thought: This is how a woman breathes when she delivers. I thought: This is how we breathe after giving birth, and the little ones look just as yellow and sick when they're born as the newly born volcano looks ugly and sick with its yellow glow. The land gives birth just like we give birth. And that was when I saw how the volcano was lighting up the night with its glow and the fires coming out of it, and I understood that everything was fine despite the pain because that is how it is to give birth. I saw the blaze coming out of the volcano and the light bursting out of it and they were beautiful in the dark of the night. And just like those beautiful bursts can be dangerous, danger can come from the children we birth.

The Father had asked us to bring the saints and we carried them among many of us. The only one who carried a skull adorned like Santa Muerte was the curandera. I thought: That's her way, if someone says light, she says darkness, because darkness is her nature. I am a midwife, I brought mine and others' into this world, and everyone knows she has ways to make sure little ones are not born. She was the only one who walked the exodus alone, without a pack, clutching that skull adorned like a saint, with its black eyes. She was also the only one who didn't talk with the others, she marched along as silent as death. They say she stopped speaking after her father was killed in front of her.

Some of the animals died from the smoke that came from the volcano's muzzle. A person died from the smoke too. His family carried his body to the camp. As the earth thundered from below, the way boiling oil thunders at drops of water, as we listened to the hot earth thundering on our exodus, a rumor began to spread that the curandera had made a deal with the devil, but I thought: Bernarda, her fires in tins couldn't cause a head cold, much less split the earth in two. But the curandera almost never speaks, she just makes her shapes with fire, and I think this is why people are more frightened of her than they are of the volcano that drove us from our homes. The land can be dangerous. She looks gentle, but she can be cruel.

Darkness has its fortunes, so the volcano that sent us on our exodus carried with it more coins than we'd ever gathered between the two towns. We were poor, but the volcano put food in our mouths. It found its way into our hearts, even, with its smoke and its glow and the way it made the night beautiful. That was why I wasn't afraid to look at it during our exodus, but Demetrio never turned around. We were frightened when the newly born volcano appeared near our milpa, right on our doorstep, because it appeared just like that and drove us all from our town. But it brought coins to us all, especially to the curandera, who got more than anyone because people said that her circles of fire had drawn fire from the earth. They said: That woman can do anything. And she was the one who became famous, they came to see her the way they came to see the volcano. More fame for the curandera than for the dangerous land.

Demetrio was invited to this, that, and the other university on the other side, he tried to sell the volcano to whatever gringo would listen, because it had been born on our doorstep, but Demetrio couldn't sell water in a drought. And then he came back and went around with the tourists who spoke in different languages, because he'd learned a few words on the other side, and he would say, "*Sank iu*" and "*Hau dew iu dew*," just like he'd been born there on the other side, and no one understood a word he said, but they were polite, you know, and they smiled because they were impressed by what was in front of them, not skinny Demetrio but instead the newly born volcano, the one that destroyed everything.

I made a journey to speak on the telephone with my boy who lives on the other side, and my grandson asked me if volcanos talked in stone. And I thought: Yes, the volcano is telling us something with its rocks. I also thought: We understand what the earth tells us when it speaks in water, in soil and seed, in trees and chayotes and squash and avocados, but not when it speaks in burning stone. One day I got close to the volcano's rumble, which Demetrio said was like the rumble of the tornado that had held him captive as a child, and he said that the earth and the wind are equals in their rage. Demetrio never stopped talking about how the tract was ours, and more words came out of him than burning stone from the volcano, because he might be skinny but he's a bottomless pit. And so money came in every day, with Demetrio telling what happened on our land with all the words that came out of him, and every day was like Christmas for us.

The tourists arrived and offered us tips for bringing them to the volcano and helping them with their photographs and videos, because some of them arrived with cameras to show the volcano in the parts of the world they were from. They left clothing, objects, they came from all over to see it. They wrote news reports about it in different languages, made videos, took photographs, they did all kinds of things to the volcano, and for all that they left money, so much that I thought: The volcano also spits out coins. I also thought: They are taking money from the rageful land. Many people questioned the will of God our Lord, but I thought: God exists, and just as He creates He also destroys, just like the volcano that destroyed everything we had. It took our land from us and our town, and in return it gave us so many coins we could have made another hill next to the volcano of nothing but coins. There were those who wished another two or three volcanos would be born so they could gather even more coins, but who cares more about coins than about the land?

REFT OF A NATION

by MAHOGANY L. BROWNE

Q. When do you know your country is a question unanswered? [1]

Q. Can water clean a history?

No. This water cannot rinse the blood from our streets.
   It is too heavy with lead.

---

1. the moment a ghost of an immigrant whispers / or / we realize this country ain't gone give us no freedom // freedom ain't nothing but a word / ain't nothing but a pretty song / in the key of an anthem that ain't ours / the moment we learn liberation ain't ours / unless we are willing to demand it / decolonize for it // unless we are willing to lose our own selves for it / unless we are willing to lose our place in the capitalism of things / order in the room / the court / the womb / got a flag planted in it // unless we walk through the

valley of the damned / slice the air with more than intentions / pledge allegiance to the end of politics and patriarchy / pledge allegiance to the end of state-sanctioned death / be uncomfortable for it / be uncomfortable in it / picket line uncrossed / until we obligate our last breath to the justice of our murdered and mistreated / until we gift the new world an accountability plan / Black dawn ordained / with the nectar of equity / until we relocate a jury who ain't our peers / watch them lose teeth and sleep over the babies murdered for practice / watch them lose weight over crime reports / faulty pipes / invisible borders erected in the likeness of small men / garden soil turned graveyard / a lecture in divisibility // when we / begin to walk around with our hands cloaked / face mask on / the real color of reckless / Black and alive / Brown and alive / Indigenous and alive / Trans and othered and alive / poor and disabled and still people—living / eyes gleaming / like the prayers they choose to forget / these poems be in the business of getting dirty // watch the ghosts and duppies and spirits rise / watch our ancestors return to plunder the earth of spilled salt genealogy / these poems are just a time stamp // a righteous light // a place-holder // a touchstone of what irrational fears can steal /// liberation ain't ours / unless we are willing to demand it / decolonize for it // unless we are willing to lose our own selves for it / unless we are willing to lose / ain't no room in capitalism for the healthy / and the womb still got a flag planted in it /// (ain't you scared?)

AN UNLUCKY MAN

by SAMANTA SCHWEBLIN
translated by MEGAN McDOWELL

THE DAY I TURNED eight, my sister—who absolutely always had to be the center of attention—swallowed an entire cup of bleach. Abi was three. First she smiled, maybe a little disgusted at the nasty taste; then her face crumpled in a frightened grimace of pain. When Mom saw the empty cup hanging from Abi's hand, she turned as white as my sister.

"Abi-my-god" was all Mom said. "Abi-my-god," and it took her a few seconds longer to spring into action.

She shook Abi by the shoulders, but my sister didn't respond. She yelled, but Abi still didn't react. She ran to the phone and called Dad, and when she came running back Abi was still standing there, the cup just dangling from her hand. Mom grabbed the cup and threw it into the sink. She opened the fridge, took out the milk, and poured a glass. She stood looking at the glass, then looked at Abi, then back at the glass, and finally dropped the glass into the sink as well. Dad worked very close by and got home quickly, but Mom still had time to do the whole show with the glass of milk again before he pulled up in the car and started honking the horn and yelling.

Mom lit out of the house like lightning with Abi clutched to her chest. The front door, the gate, and the car doors were all flung open. There was more horn honking and Mom, who was already sitting in the car, started to cry. Dad had to shout at me twice before I understood that I was the one who was supposed to close up.

We drove the first ten blocks in less time than it had taken me to close the car door and fasten my seat belt. But when we got to the main avenue, the traffic was practically stopped. Dad honked the horn and shouted out the window, "We have to get to the hospital! We have to get to the hospital!" The cars around us maneuvered and miraculously let us pass, but a couple cars ahead, we had to start the whole operation over again. Dad braked in the traffic, stopped honking, and pounded his head against the steering wheel. I had never seen him do such a thing. There was a moment of silence, and then he sat up and looked at me in the rearview mirror. He turned around and said to me:

"Take off your underpants."

I was wearing my school uniform. All my underwear was white, but I wasn't exactly thinking about that just then, and I couldn't understand Dad's request. I pressed my hands into the seat to support myself better. I looked at Mom and she shouted:

"Take off your damned underpants!"

I took them off. Dad grabbed them out of my hands. He rolled down the window, went back to honking, and started waving my underpants out the window. He raised them high while he yelled and kept honking, and it seemed like everyone on the avenue turned around to look at them. My underpants were small, but they were also very white. An ambulance a block behind us turned on its siren, caught up with us quickly, and started clearing a path. Dad kept on waving the underpants until we reached the hospital.

They parked the car by the ambulances and jumped out. Without waiting, Mom took Abi and ran straight into the hospital. I wasn't sure whether I should get out or not: I didn't have any underpants on and I looked around to see where Dad had left them, but they weren't on the seat or in his hand, which was already slamming his car door behind him.

"Come on, come on," said Dad.

He opened my door and helped me out. He gave my shoulder a few pats as we walked into the emergency room. Mom came through a doorway at the back and signaled to us. I was relieved to see she was talking again, giving explanations to the nurses.

"Stay here," said Dad, and he pointed to some orange chairs on the other side of the main waiting area.

I sat. Dad went into the consulting room with Mom and I waited for a while. I don't know how long, but it felt long. I pressed my knees together tightly and thought about everything that had happened so quickly, and about the possibility that any of the kids from school had seen the spectacle with my underpants. When I sat up straight, my jumper rode up and my bare bottom touched part of the plastic seat. Sometimes the nurse came in or out of the consulting room and I could hear my parents arguing. At one point I craned my neck and caught a glimpse of Abi moving restlessly on one of the cots, and I knew that, at least today, she wasn't going to die. And I still had to wait.

Then a man came and sat down next to me. I don't know where he came from; I hadn't noticed him before.

"How's it going?" he asked.

I thought about saying *very well*, which is what Mom always said if someone asked her that, even if she'd just told me and my sister that we were driving her insane.

"Okay," I said.

"Are you waiting for someone?"

I thought about it. I wasn't really waiting for anyone; at least, it wasn't what I wanted to be doing right then. So I shook my head, and he said:

"Why are you sitting in the waiting room, then?"

I understood it was a great contradiction. He opened a small bag he had on his lap and rummaged in it a bit, unhurried. Then he took a pink slip of paper from his wallet.

"Here it is. I knew I had it somewhere."

The paper was printed with the number 92.

"It's good for an ice cream cone. My treat," he said.

I told him no. You shouldn't accept things from strangers.

"But it's free. I won it."

"No." I looked straight ahead and we sat in silence.

"Suit yourself," he said, without getting angry.

He took a magazine from his bag and started to fill in a crossword puzzle. The door to the consulting room opened again and I heard Dad say, "I will not condone such nonsense." That's Dad's clincher for ending almost any argument. The man sitting next to me didn't seem to hear it.

"It's my birthday," I said.

It's my birthday, I repeated to myself. What should I do?

The man held the pen to mark his place in a box on the puzzle and looked at me in surprise. I nodded without looking at him, aware I had his attention again.

"But...," he said, and he closed the magazine. "Sometimes I just don't understand women. If it's your birthday, what are you doing in a hospital waiting room?"

He was an observant man. I straightened up again in my seat and I saw that, even then, I barely came up to his shoulders. He smiled and I smoothed my hair. And then I said:

"I'm not wearing any underpants."

I don't know why I said it. It's just that it was my birthday and I wasn't wearing underpants, and I couldn't stop thinking about those circumstances. He was still looking at me. Maybe he was startled or offended, and I understood that, although it hadn't been my intention, there was something vulgar about what I had just said.

"But it's your birthday," he said.

I nodded.

"It's not fair. A person can't just go around without underpants when it's their birthday."

"I know," I said emphatically, because now I understood just how Abi's whole display was a personal affront to me.

He sat for a moment without saying anything. Then he glanced toward the big windows that looked out onto the parking lot.

"I know where to get you some underpants," he said.

"Where?"

"Problem solved." He stowed his things and stood up.

I hesitated. Precisely because I wasn't wearing underpants, but also because I didn't know if he was telling the truth. He looked toward the front desk and waved one hand at the attendants.

"We'll be right back," he said, and he pointed to me. "It's her birthday." And then I thought, Oh, please, Jesus, don't let him say anything about my underpants, but he didn't: he opened the door and winked at me, and then I knew I could trust him.

We went out to the parking lot. Standing, I came up to a little above his waist. Dad's car was still next to the ambulances, and a policeman was circling it, annoyed. I kept looking over at the policeman, and he watched us walk away. The breeze wrapped around my legs and rose, making a tent out of my uniform. I had to hold it down while I walked, keeping my legs awkwardly close together.

He turned around to see if I was following him, and he saw me fighting with my skirt.

"We'd better stick close to the wall."

"I want to know where we're going."

"Don't get persnickety with me now, darling."

We crossed the avenue and went into a shopping center. It was an uninviting place, and I was pretty sure Mom didn't go there. We walked to the back toward a big clothing store, a truly huge one that I don't think Mom had ever been to, either. Before we went in he said to me, "Don't get lost," and gave me his hand, which was cold and very soft. He waved to the cashiers the same way he waved to the desk attendants when we'd left the hospital, but no one responded. We walked down the aisles. In addition to dresses, pants, and shirts, there were work clothes: hard hats, yellow overalls like the ones trash collectors wear, smocks for cleaning ladies, plastic boots, and even some tools. I wondered if he bought his clothes there and if he would use any of those things in his job, and then I also wondered what his name was.

"Here we are," he said.

We were surrounded by tables of underwear for men and women. If I reached out, I could touch a large bin full of giant underpants, bigger than any I'd seen before, and they were only three pesos each. With one of those pairs of underpants, they could have made three for someone my size.

"Not those," he said. "Here." And he led me a little farther, to a section with smaller sizes. "Look at all the underpants they have. Which will you choose, my lady?"

I looked around a little. Almost all of them were white or pink. I pointed to a white pair, one of the few that didn't have a bow on them.

"These," I said. "But I can't pay for them."

He came a little closer and said into my ear:

"That doesn't matter."

"Are you the owner?"

"No. It's your birthday."

I smiled.

"But we have to find better ones. We need to be sure."

"Okay, darling," I ventured.

"Don't say 'darling,'" he said. "I'll get persnickety." And he imitated me holding down my skirt in the parking lot.

He made me laugh. When he finished clowning around, he held

out two closed fists, and he stayed just like that until I understood; I touched the right one. He opened it: it was empty.

"You can still choose the other one."

I touched the other one. It took me a moment to realize it was a pair of underpants, because I had never seen black ones before. And they were for girls because they had white hearts on them, so small they looked like dots, and Hello Kitty's face was on the front, right where there was usually that bow that Mom and I don't like at all.

"You'll have to try them on," he said.

I held the underpants to my chest. He gave me his hand again and we went toward the changing rooms, which looked empty. We peered in. He said he didn't know if he could go in with me, because they were for women only. He said I would have to go alone. It was logical because, unless it's someone you know very well, it's not good for people to see you in your underpants. But I was afraid of going into the dressing room alone. Or something worse: coming out and not seeing him there.

"What's your name?" I asked.

"I can't tell you that."

"Why not?"

He knelt down. Then he was almost my height, or maybe I was a couple inches taller.

"Because I'm cursed."

"Cursed? What's cursed?"

"A woman who hates me said that the next time I say my name, I'm going to die."

I thought it might be another joke, but he said it very seriously.

"You could write it down for me."

"Write it down?"

"If you wrote it, you wouldn't say it: you'd be writing it. And if I know your name, I can call for you and I won't be so scared to go into the dressing room alone."

"But we can't be sure. What if this woman thinks writing my name is the same as saying it? What if by saying it, she meant letting someone else know, letting my name out into the world in any way?"

"But how would she know?"

"People don't trust me, and I'm the unluckiest man in the world."

"I don't believe you. There's no way she'd find out."

"I know what I'm talking about."

Together, we looked at the underpants in my hands. I thought my parents might be finished by now.

"But it's my birthday," I said.

And maybe I did it on purpose. At the time I felt like I did: my eyes filled with tears. Then he hugged me. It was a very fast movement; he crossed his arms behind my back and squeezed me so tight my face pressed into his chest. Then he let me go, took out his magazine and pen, and wrote something on the right edge of the cover. Then he tore it off and folded it three times before handing it to me.

"Don't read it," he said, and he stood up and pushed me gently toward the dressing room.

I passed four empty cubicles. Before gathering my courage and entering the fifth, I put the paper into the pocket of my jumper and turned to look at him, and we smiled at each other.

I tried on the underpants. They were perfect. I lifted up my jumper so I could see just how good they looked. They were so, so very perfect. They fit incredibly well, and because they were black, Dad would never ask me for them so he could wave them out the window behind the ambulance. And even if he did, I wouldn't be so embarrassed if my classmates saw. *Just look at the underpants that girl has*, they'd all think. *Now, those are some perfect underpants.*

I realized I couldn't take them off now. And I realized something else: They didn't have a security tag. They had a little mark where the tag would usually go, but there was no alarm. I stood a moment longer looking at myself in the mirror, and then I couldn't stand it anymore and I took out the little paper, opened it, and read it.

I came out of the dressing room and he wasn't where I had left him, but then I saw him a little farther away, next to the bathing suits. He looked at me, and when he saw I wasn't carrying the underpants, he winked, and I was the one who took his hand. This time he held on to me tighter; we walked together toward the exit.

I trusted that he knew what he was doing, that a cursed man who had the world's worst luck knew how to do these things. We passed the line of registers at the main entrance. One of the security guards glanced at us and adjusted his belt. He would surely think the nameless man was my dad, and I felt proud.

We passed the sensors at the exit and went into the mall, and we kept walking in silence all the way back to the avenue. That was when I saw Abi, alone, in the middle of the hospital parking lot. And I saw Mom, on our side of the street, looking around frantically. Dad was also coming toward us from the parking lot. He was following fast behind the policeman who'd been looking at our car before, and who was now pointing at us. Everything happened very quickly. Dad saw us, yelled my name, and a few seconds later that policeman and two others who came out of nowhere were on top of us. The unlucky man let go of me, but I held my hand suspended toward him for a few seconds. They surrounded him and shoved him roughly. They asked what he was doing, they asked his name, but he didn't answer. Mom hugged me and checked me over from head to toe. She had my white underpants dangling from her right hand. Then, patting me all over, she noticed I was wearing a different pair. She lifted my jumper in a single movement: it was such a rude and vulgar thing to do, right there in front of everyone, that I jerked away and had to take a few steps backward to keep from falling down. The unlucky man looked at me and I looked at him. When Mom saw the black underpants, she screamed, "Son of a bitch, son of a bitch," and Dad lunged at him and tried to punch him. The cops moved to separate them.

I fished for the paper in my jumper pocket, put it in my mouth, and as I swallowed it I repeated his name in silence, several times, so I would never forget it.

WORLDLY
WONDERS

by SABRINA HELEN LI

THE SERIES I STAR in is called "Human China: Eat Me. Love Me."
Over the course of thirty minutes, a cast of four naked Asian girls
assemble themselves into a real, live porcelain bowl. I am the leader,
the star of the performance, the base of the bowl. To be a good
bowl, you need to make the fullest part of yourself hollow. I turn
my stomach into a weighty thing. I never knew that strength was
required to be hollow, that stamina was needed to be empty. It is
necessary that we hold our bodies, contorting them for ten minutes
at a time to give our customers an optimal experience. Our customers would rather see Worldly Wonders' versions of countries
than the actual countries themselves. As a theme park, Worldly
Wonders has ensured that each country has its own monument,
town, and restaurant. The countries stand pressed together like toy

soldiers, erected in a tight circle around the perimeter of a private island that was once a golf course for business tycoons. In the back of air-conditioned rickshaws, our visitors quietly travel the world. I am Chinese, so that means I can be a geisha, a sumo wrestler, a hibachi chef, a silk dancer. The park has made sure each staff member is an authority on their country's customs. No question is too stupid. No question is unanswerable.

On a cold wooden table, three other girls now lie naked on their sides, their bodies coiled against mine, stretched like worms. They form the walls of the bowl. Only the center of my spine touches the floor. I hold the rest of my body in midair, in a tight half crunch. I cradle my body as if I were my own baby. An artist proceeds to airbrush us white. He draws cracks on our bodies. The ones we already have are never the ones he wants. He always likes to give us new places to be broken. The artist draws blue flowers and dragons, tight tendrils of cloud. The same syrupy blue inside my biology textbooks from high school—blue blood, a blue that comes only from never being exposed to air, so hidden within the body that it becomes something else. I used to think it was magical. In middle school, I would pull my skin tight like saran wrap, holding myself to the light, hoping I could see something underneath. I was devastated when my mother told me that human blood isn't blue—it's just drawn that way to make sure we don't mistake it for something else.

What makes Worldly Wonders special is its interactive series. When planning China's series, the creative director wanted it to be something different. The director wanted a performance that was lighthearted, fun. Americans never really think of violence when they think of the Chinese. And if they do, it's never a guilty violence, a complicit violence. My friends Josh and Sam work in Mexico and Africa. They like to tell me how lucky I am.

The thing that upsets me the most about our series isn't the customers or the staff. It's that the girls and I, the four of us, never say anything to one another after our performance. We disconnect our limbs from one another and head to the showers. In the shower, the white paint comes off us in patches. We turn the water milky, sour and curdled. The girls and I then disperse and quietly walk back to our rooms. It would be nice if we could all somehow be friends.

A month into our series, the director wants us to try out a new formation. The body painter arranges the other girls' faces to be on the inside of the bowl rather than the outside. I look up and I see their faces staggered above mine. Today, they are allowed to close their eyes. A Worldly Wonders staff member dressed as a waiter walks the next group of customers, a family of three, into the back room of the restaurant where our performance takes place. I hear them take their seats around the table and start to whisper while they wait for their meal. We are set right in front of them, exactly three feet away. The waiter proceeds to scoop hot rice into our curved limbs. He continues to fill our bowl with shredded beef, thick noodles, three plump eggs. He tosses it all together with a pair of giant chopsticks, and I watch the girls above me wince in pain. I dart my tongue out and snatch a grain of rice into my mouth and swallow. I wonder if we change the taste of the food at all. The first thing anyone does when they are presented with the bowl is search for our eyes. I never know where to look. I don't know if it makes me more or less powerful to stare back at them. I imagine my grandmother slurping tea from me, seeing my face, turning the bowl around, and continuing to drink.

Being at the bottom of the bowl, I get the brunt of the heat. It's hard for me to breathe for those ten minutes. I have to eat some of the food myself, create a pocket of oxygen and bury my face in it. My face is positioned so the customer always sees me when they're done eating. I am the surprise, the free toy at the bottom of the box. I watch their faces hover over mine, their jowls stuffed with food. Their many chins hanging downward. Nobody ever talks to me when I'm a bowl. Today I am staring into the eyes of a small boy. He gets up on a chair and leans into the bowl, bringing his face closer and closer to mine. He touches my nose with his finger, and after a moment of hesitation, the boy bites the tip of it. The paint comes off, and a square of my skin, pale and red, stares back at him like an open window. I wonder if one day he'll want to climb inside it. I look at his mouth and I try to find where the white paint has gone. It must have disappeared between his teeth. The boy smiles at me, licking his lips. "Daddy, come here! Look what I did."

I am not allowed to scream. I open my mouth and make sure nothing comes out. I hear the father walking toward the table. He looks down at me, my mouth open, my nose red, and he pulls his son from his seat. I hear a slap. I close my eyes. "But she's a bowl!" the son yells. The father doesn't respond. There is only shuffling. When I open my eyes again, the father has taken the boy's place. He now stares deep into my eyes, just as his son did. He brings his head closer and closer to mine, rice catching on his sleeves. I try to hold my face still. I try to stare back. I wonder where the mother is. I wish she would come and see me too. Suddenly, the father is speaking to me. He asks if I have a name. I've never been asked to speak before as a bowl, but before I can respond the waiter interrupts us. He says the next customers are ready to dine at our restaurant. He tells the family of three that their meal now needs to be over. At the end of the performance, visitors are led into the gift shop. There you can purchase a plaster replica of us to take home with you. Once, as a joke, Sam and Josh bought one and slurped their lunch from my body. "Look, they even made you heat resistant," Josh said, laughing. With his pinky held out, Sam brought his lips to the edge. I saw my head disappear into his mouth as he licked the bottom of the bowl. I smashed it on the ground and watched myself crack in all the wrong places.

After that, I imagined hundreds of American cupboards filled with miniature casts of my body, pieced together with other Asian bodies, forming something to be filled. I imagined the man who would one day be my husband eating from my body before he'd even seen it. Is this how I will be remembered? How will I explain this to my children? I'm most afraid to have a son.

I always take my lunch break with Sam and Josh. Today we are in Mexico. Josh has just finished his shift. Five years ago, Mexico's interactive series was based on La Llorona. An old woman with long hair would go running through the park with ten plastic baby dolls dangling from a thin string around her neck and wail into the faces of visitors. People would throw coins at her, not knowing what else to do. After 2016, though, Worldly Wonders consulted with a cultural sensitivity expert on how to stay relevant. It added a giant cage in the center of Mexico. The woman who played La Llorona would plant baby dolls throughout the park before her performance, and as the visitors watched, she would scurry around, finding each doll she had meticulously hidden. La Llorona would fling the dolls into the cage, their bodies quietly bouncing off one another. Sometimes in mid-flight, a head would separate from a neck, a hollow arm from a cotton torso, and they would roll through a small hole in the cage until they were stopped by a real child's foot. Nobody knew what to do. Sam works in Africa. There are no countries in Africa, just the continent. Africa's interactive series has stayed the same for decades. Every day, visitors can experience becoming enslaved. They are shuttled onto a single wooden ship. By night, each visitor has been awarded the prize of setting themselves free.

At the end of each day, Josh, Sam, and I come together on the roof of my pagoda to watch the visitors' pale bodies exit through the park gates, their backs always hunched, their mouths taut, their legs heavy with the three-hour obstacle they paid to face today. Worldly Wonders says the goal of its series is to educate, to transform.

"Have your customers been tipping you less lately?" Josh asks during a lunch break. We shake our heads no. We're sitting under a giant sombrero and the shade feels nice. "The director better get involved. I swear. Three years of this shit, and for what?"

I bite down on my burrito. "I don't know. We're introducing our visitors to new cultures, right? We're teaching people, getting them interested. I'm not saying we're saints or anything, but I think we're doing something good." The boys are silent, and my cheeks turn red and rough. Sam looks at me for a long time, his tortilla turning soggy.

"Getting them interested in what, exactly? The second I find a job that pays better than this, I'm out of here."

Josh rolls his eyes. Every other week, Sam talks about leaving. Sam has been working at Worldly Wonders the longest of the three of us. He saw Worldly Wonders at its start—a collection of museums and dioramas where visitors could kill a few hours. Sam was its first hire, Africa its first interactive series. The park wanted to give visitors a reason to stay the night. A desire to stay forever. Most can afford to visit Worldly Wonders for a couple of hours, but it's only the richest who can stay here for days, for weeks. They want to learn more from us, they say. They're growing to love us, they say. Some of these special visitors even date the employees. The special visitors stay in the best suites in our hotel next to the park. Every night they wait for someone to come join them. One special visitor got married to Elizabeth from Japan last month. They now have a home together in real Switzerland. The regulars sometimes ask the director if they can live in the park with us, but it's against the rules. Those rules, the director says, are meant to protect us.

I would never tell Josh or Sam this, but it's nice to be considered an authority on something. Every day visitors come up and ask me questions: "Do you like living in China? Are your homes big or small? Is your country as powerful as people say it is? Are you really that obedient? Are you really that smart? Do you think men could like me as much as they like you? Do you think they could ever like me more?" I feel the most Asian when I am working. I'm never mistaken for anything else. People want only my answers. My answers are the only ones that matter.

When I was five, I tried to teach myself how to be Chinese. I woke up every Sunday morning at 6 a.m. to watch anime. I taught myself how to cook rice and dumplings and packed them in my lunchbox every day before school. I bought ancient Chinese scrolls on eBay and hung them in my room, not knowing what the characters meant. Every weekend, I put on performances for my grandma, my whole family huddled around her kitchen table. I only knew how to say the races in Shanghainese. I was able to pronounce those the best, listing them with quick confidence: ha ning, ba ning, zhong guo ning, ing du ning. My grandmother would always laugh. "So you do know what we're saying? I don't have to translate for you after all."

My mother never liked it when I performed. She said I spoke everything as if it were a song. She says I must have learned that from my dad.

My mother at one point did consider enrolling me in Chinese school. But with her Mandarin so broken and mine nonexistent, she knew I would never really learn the language, that I would always be behind, that each Saturday morning I'd go to my desk and there would always be someone more Chinese sitting next to me. I wish she had let me go. I imagine whispering to my grandma in a language my mother can't speak. I picture my mother alone and mute in a corner, calling out to us like a dying bird: *What are you saying? Tell me what you're saying.* It is my ugliest desire.

* * *

On Tuesdays, my ex-boyfriend Caleb visits me. We broke up a year ago, but for the past two months, he's started coming to the park again. He broke up with me because I don't read the news as much as he thinks I should. He says it's a person's civic duty to be as informed as possible: he's memorized the exact number of people who have suffered the effects of gun violence, the exact number of bombs the US drops around the world each day. He reads the news at dinner, at parties, right after sex. He's never said so, but he thinks I'm not political. Caleb shows up because he is sad and lonely and doesn't think those are smart or effective things to feel.

We sit in my room at the top of the glass pagoda. Today I'm trying a new act out on him. Worldly Wonders wants each country to have its own museum. To save money, the director asked me to build the China exhibit myself. He asked me to bring in objects from my own life. I looked around my small bedroom to decide what to excavate. I picked out a pot of fake plastic orchids, a photo of my grandmother, and a small knife that I'm not sure how I got. Now I place them neatly in a row. Before I came to Worldly Wonders, I was in acting school. This is by far the hardest job I've had. This is the only job I could get. I think being at Worldly Wonders is the best exercise. I am always in character. I wonder if Caleb's started to notice. I wonder if that means I'm doing a good job.

"Once upon a time," I begin, "in the land of China, people learned not to trust the food they were given. Nobody knows why this was. But it was unquestioned. The only way the Chinese knew to remedy this problem was to grow their own gardens. My great-great-grandmother started the first garden in our family, which would then be passed on to my grandmother and then to my mother and then, one day, to me. Supposedly, the original seeds are still used to this day. The most delicious food is grown from these plots of land. Each family has its own special touch. You can tell from the taste."

I don't know where this story is coming from exactly, but I'd like to think it's true—that it comes from deep within me, some sort of memory I was born into.

"Well, what do you think?" I ask after I'm done.

"Shouldn't you be talking about China's history? Isn't this bigger than just you? You should be telling people about the Sino-Japanese Wars, the Cultural Revolution, Tiananmen Square. You could really change some people's minds."

"That's all just violence. Why would I tell them about that?"

Caleb just looks at me. "Is any of it even real? History is how you educate people. Not what you're doing all day—getting naked, bending yourself into a bowl. What kind of message do you think that's sending?"

I ask him to leave. I sit alone with my objects. In the apartment we shared, I used to stare out the window and watch Caleb's small body walk into the distance and then wait hours for it to reemerge. Caleb feels most included when he's in a crowd. He'll sometimes go off walking by himself just to find one. Caleb doesn't invite me places. I've never met his friends. He's never even invited me to go walking with him. Caleb wouldn't admit it, but he often joins marches without knowing what they're protesting. It goes without saying that my ex-boyfriend thinks my job is stupid. He says it is propaganda.

I've never been to a protest. My parents have never protested. We are a quiet family with quiet jobs and quiet desires. Alone in the pagoda, I try to make a list of all the things I care about. I make lists for my mother and father. I move my finger down all three of our lists. There is nothing there that I'd march for. I stare at my computer screen. It hums against my skin. I don't actually know what my parents want. I wonder if desire is something that can be learned. I wonder if I can teach myself. I hear a knock on my door. It's Caleb. Behind the glow of his phone, he mumbles that he can't go back home.

There is a virus. Quiet and spreading. It came to us from China, the real China. The virus, like most things, travels through touch. The news tells us the virus can live for hours on surfaces. I learn that my body is a surface. The news instructs us not to touch ourselves, let alone one another. There are already fifty cases in New York, seventy-two in California. Because Worldly Wonders is on such a remote island, the disease hasn't reached us. The director promises it never will. The director encourages us to go about our days normally. Thousands of people now want to journey to Worldly Wonders. The hundreds of people who are already here don't want to leave. The park director tries to capitalize on this immediately. Bottles of water skyrocket to twenty dollars each, a roll of toilet paper to sixteen. The park prints new brochures and changes the website—visitors, if they have the money, can live in the park for as long as they want. Three quick marriages happen the night of the director's announcement. Three lucky girls get promoted from performers to wives, and with their new status, their belongings are seamlessly moved into special suites. The girls disappear into the night, and I never see or hear from them again.

Right now, the only thing Worldly Wonders is worried about is how the public will respond to the park allowing its own China to remain open. "Our China is different, though. Better. Ours is a clean and pure China. Let's keep it that way," the park director says in an email to the staff. The real reason the director wants to keep China, though, is that "Human China: Eat Me, Love Me" is its best seller, one of its main draws.

Today I walk to the restaurant in China and get ready to perform. I assemble myself into a bowl with the other girls. The waiters let the visitors in, and as usual, they eat from us. I watch their faces lower toward us. For the first time, I see someone who is scared to eat from me. I close my eyes and think of that father who stared down at me. I wonder what he told his son after they left the room. Did he tell his son I was beautiful? That I tasted nice? That if he grew up big and strong, maybe one day he could marry a girl like me? I tell myself that what I saw in that father's eyes was love. I think he is a good man. I wonder if he could adopt me as his daughter. I imagine playing with his son, turning into a bowl at his command. I imagine hiding from his wife. I imagine the father asking me to forget my past family, my past home. I think I'd be able stay with him as long as I liked. I think I'd be good at obeying.

I open my eyes and see the new visitor still standing above me, bobbing his head. I take a deep breath and try not to move. He picks the noodles off my body and blows on them, cleaning them. I watch his spit fly from his mouth, and I feel it land on me. He tentatively bites the noodle before dropping it back into the bowl. It falls on my eye, and it's hard for me to see. He steps back. "Whatever," the man mumbles to his friends. "Let them keep my money."

As I'm leaving that day, I overhear one of the girls quitting. Sarah has worked at the park for eight years. She talks to the director. I see her pointing at us. "Can I at least be moved to a different part of Asia? I am not even Chinese." The director shakes his head, and Sarah leaves on the next boat. Sarah doesn't want to touch us anymore. She thinks we're too much of a risk. She doesn't know where our bodies have been. I stand next to the two other girls, both actually Chinese. We look at one another. I distance myself from them. None of us have seen our families in the months since the tourist season started. I don't even know if any of their families have visited the real China recently. But someone needs to be blamed.

The park director tells us not to talk about the news with the visitors. The director says he thinks of us as a family, children he has meticulously adopted and, therefore, saved. A lot of the visitors tell me to go back to China when they see me walking throughout the park. The director tells me to take this literally, so with my head hung low, I slowly march back to China. The director tells us to listen to the visitors, that we should go back to any country they say we're from. A day later, I run into my coworkers from Japan and Korea. We all walk back to China together.

Josh and Sam won't come to China to see me. We meet underneath the sombrero. I bring dumplings for lunch, but they say they're too full. I ask them if they notice anything different about the park. They tell me that fewer people have been participating in the interactive series—they have enough danger in their lives now. But the visitors who do participate are angrier. They use the series as a way to corner the workers, to force Josh and Sam to talk longer with them. One guy filled a water gun with hand sanitizer and started shooting at them during their performances. It burned their eyes and skin. They show me the marks.

I don't know how to comfort them. I feel like some of this has to be my fault. I feel bad now, telling them what's making me upset.

"Nobody wants to eat from me anymore."

Josh and Sam are silent for a bit. Finally, Josh speaks. "Isn't that—well—good?"

"Yeah, I guess it is." I wonder if Worldly Wonders will stop selling my bowls at the gift shop. I wonder if the park will throw them away. "Hey, maybe the director will let you guys eat from me for free now. You can come by China and see it for yourselves."

Josh shakes his head. "No, it's okay. We respect you too much to do that."

I call my mother that night. I haven't called her since I started at Worldly Wonders. She doesn't know what my job is, exactly, so I tell her I'm a waitress at a popular Chinese restaurant in the park. I tell her the guests don't want to eat my food anymore, and it makes me sad. My mother is silent for a long time. "Sometimes they spit their food out at me," I add. "They like to aim for my eyes when I serve it to them." I hear the phone crackle, and then my mother's voice comes out clear and precise. "Do they ever hit you?" No. "Do they ever steal anything from you?" No. "Are they no longer paying for their food?" No. "Are they going to shoot you?" No. Before I can say anything more, she hangs up the phone.

*　*　*

The first case appears in Worldly Wonders Italy. Everyone turns to China, though. One person out of the fifteen who are sick in Italy claims to have eaten from "Human China." It takes five days after the first park outbreak of the virus for "Human China: Eat Me. Love Me" to get pulled. They say we contaminated the food. They say the Chinese bodies must have done something to it. How can you trust a bowl that is not as hollow as it should be, that is not as quiet and pure as it claims, that is human after all?

The director sends out an apology email to all the guests and staff. He stops whatever pop song is playing over the loudspeakers and reads it out so the whole park can hear it. He says nobody has anything to fear, that all of Italy is now being quarantined, that the rest of our wonderful world is safe and sound.

I tell Caleb that part of me misses being a bowl. The two of us are afraid to go outside, so we stay in my room. I tell him more things about myself than I intend to. There isn't much to do, so we have sex a lot. Caleb is silent as he fucks me. He never says out loud what he wants. To be fair, I've never asked. Caleb bites my ear, and without meaning to, I feel my body harden and transform into a bowl. My stomach goes stiff. His face hovers above mine and my body lurches toward him, the center of my spine stuck on the bed. I stretch and stretch toward him, and I hold myself like that, hollow. Some of his sweat drips onto my stomach and collects there. A tiny little puddle, a barely-there pool. I feel it slosh around on my skin, and

I hold myself taut, making sure none of it leaks, that all of it is safe and secure, like a good little bowl would do.

His head falls onto my stomach, crashes into the little bowl I had been keeping safe. "What is that? Is that from you or me?" he asks as he wipes his face. Before I can answer, he slaps my stomach. He hits it again and again, trying to remove whatever has collected inside of me. My body barely moves as he slaps me. I have gotten too good at being a bowl. Whatever is put inside of me stays there. I wish that father could see me now, that he could see how talented I have become. I bet he'd be proud of me. I'd like for him to take me home. Caleb is panting now, and more sweat drips into me. For the first time, I think I know what he wants. I'm not sure if Caleb has ever cared about making me clean before now. His brow furrows and his hand extends farther and farther back.

Suddenly I'm being lifted. Caleb holds me, cradles me like a baby as he walks me to the tub. Without warning, he turns my body, unhinges it from his, and I swing open, carelessly and wide, like a broken door. The liquid tumbles out of my stomach, and Caleb sighs with relief, happy with himself. He places me in the tub and washes me like a dish. When Caleb goes out walking later that night, he doesn't come back.

Despite there being no cases of the virus in Worldly Wonders China, the director says the Chinese girls must be quarantined separately. The park builds us a glass box and places us on the highest floor in China's main pagoda. "But I've never even been to China," I say as the director takes us away during the middle of a performance.

"I'm healthy. You have nothing to worry about." He looks at me with a small smile and says, "This is supposed to be China. You are supposed to be China. This is your job." I wonder where Caleb is. Here is something for him to protest.

Together, the two other girls and I, naked and painted, step inside the glass box. The team at Worldly Wonders has carefully thought through its construction. We have a heating system underneath our feet; an adjacent tank holds our drinking water. There are three pneumatic tubes leading to the bottom right of our box, the same transparent tubes used at banks to quickly give customers clean, crisp money. The director explains that one tube is meant for our waste, another for water, the last for food. I imagine my shit zooming across the park, visitors craning their necks, taking pictures. The director seals the box shut. Every necessity has been accounted for, he says. We never have to leave.

Lindsay is the first to speak, saying we should divide the glass box into three, so that we can all have our own uncontaminated sections. As she is the right side of the bowl, her right ankle is almost always pressed against my face. It is rough and has three deep lines. Her bones are large. I think she is from California. Anna is the left side of the bowl. Her arm is always by my neck. Her nails are short and stubby, but she always paints them black. They look even smaller than they should be. I look at the three of us. Our paint looks stupid when we're not forming a bowl—half of Lindsay's arm is painted black in an effort to make it disappear, a section of Anna's thigh is shaded round and white, there is a crack painted down the middle of my face that suddenly stops at the top of my lip because that's where Anna's arm is always resting. I can't wait until it fades.

Anna and I agree with Lindsay's proposal. We face our spines toward one another and look out toward the clear corners. The box is small. My back is almost touching theirs. One time I sneeze and I fall into them. I apologize quickly and they say nothing in response. We wait like that for an hour, cross-legged, unmoving, until the first rush of tourists comes to greet us. It's hard for us to form a bowl now. Nobody can eat from us anyway. But Worldly Wonders has already paid us for the month, and we need to earn our money somehow. I wasn't able to take my museum objects into the box, so instead I look down at myself—my dirty hands, my thin-skinned stomach, my oily hair. I assess my body and divide myself into parts. I think of the best way to present myself to my audience.

"Once upon a time, in the land of China," I begin, projecting so all can hear, "there was a girl with a dagger in her head, the blade small and thin. Her mother inserted it in her so she could always see herself. It was so expertly placed that there was no trace of blood. The girl was the wound. The blood, with nowhere to escape to, blossomed inside her, grew bouquets, bitter and sharp. Once, when she was a baby, her father gave her flowers from the garden to play with, their roots still intact. He turned away, and when he turned back, he saw that the flowers were cleanly cut. Rigid and straight. They smelled of nothing, and his daughter had never looked happier."

At night I watch the other girls sleep. I match my breathing to theirs. Our bodies curve around one another perfectly. I wonder what they're dreaming. I wonder what their families are like. I imagine Lindsay as an older sister. I imagine Anna as an only child. I imagine them living in houses similar to mine. I think of them speaking Mandarin to one another fluently, switching into the language so easily from English, using it to talk about me in secret. I sigh. I wonder what Lindsay's and Anna's mothers think about them being here, about them having these jobs. I bet their mothers are proud.

By the end of the first week, the audience edges closer to us. A man takes out his water gun full of hand sanitizer and shoots. He says he needs to protect his son. It's the father from before. The glass box is doused. Our reflections blur. The man uses up five tubs of hand sanitizer. He keeps reloading. My reflection disappears. Lindsay's and Anna's soon follow. We look at one another.

"Should we do something?" I whisper.

They don't respond.

Our bodies briefly reappear in the glass, then become erased again. I want to reach out and grab Lindsay's and Anna's hands, but instead I keep my arms at my sides and wait. I start slapping my skin whenever the man shoots. To hear a noise. To see something on my body. Something needs to come from this.

"Stop it," Anna says, not taking her eyes off the crowd. She forces my hand into hers. It's small and sweaty.

When the crowd leaves, Anna turns to me and asks, "Do you know that man?"

"He came to the show the day before the park shut down," I respond.

"Do you think he's going to hurt us?" Lindsay asks.

"No, I think he may try to help us. He even hurt his son a little to save me. It might be nice to get to know him, to have someone else who's on our side," I say.

They don't respond.

Even in our small box, I can feel them inching away from me. I hope they know I've always wanted to be on their side. I hope they know I care.

That night the father comes back to the box. He comes straight up to the glass and pulls out a plaster version of me. It's from a bowl from the gift shop downstairs: my body has been disconnected from the rest of the girls. He gets down on one knee and holds my body up to me like a present. He asks me a question in Mandarin. I ask him if he can repeat himself, and in an accent-less Mandarin he says it again.

I think he wants me to marry him, and I nod. I can't ask him to translate this for me. I know we won't actually get married, but I imagine my will-be husband speaking to my grandmother in Mandarin. My mother and I are in a dark corner together. My will-be husband translates in whispers that only I can hear—secrets my grandmother would never tell my mother. And he smiles at me, and I try to smile, and my mother, even my imaginary one, is silent. My will-be husband taps my plaster body on the glass box to get my attention once more. He says in English that he knows I'm not dirty. He was just trying to protect me from them. He points to Lindsay and Anna. He promises to get me out of there. He says he can bring me home with him. He says he will leave his wife for me, that I already have a child that can be all my own. He puts my plaster body back in his pocket and walks away. I wonder if one day he'll pass my body down to his son. I hope his real wife will break it before he ever does.

*   *   *

In the third week of our confinement, the rest of the world descends into panic. A bad storm hits most of the East Coast and takes out the electricity. All across the nation, there are blackouts, no heat, no air conditioning, very little wi-fi. Everyone is too afraid to go outside to fix anything, so the world remains in darkness. Worldly Wonders is the only place that is surviving at the moment. There is a backup generator. We are safe for now. Sam and Josh catch me up on this through the walls of the glass box. The director has recently relocated them to China, the largest uncontaminated space, since half the countries in Worldly Wonders have reported cases of the virus. The director now wants Sam and Josh to wait on the richer visitors, to get them anything they might need.

According to Sam, my parents have been trying to contact me. They tried to get into the park a couple of days ago. Back home, in New York, almost everyone is infected. The stores are closed. Upon seeing their faces at the gate, the security guards at Worldly Wonders turned my parents away. Sam says my mother kept asking if she could speak to me over the phone, if her daughter was all right. She said her daughter was an employee, a good employee, that they must be able to let her and her husband in because of that. Once Sam's done talking, I ask, "Was she crying?" No. "Was she screaming?" No. "Did she say she loved me? Did she even call me by my name?" No. I stare at Sam and he opens his mouth a couple of times and finally tells me he couldn't get her in. He promises he tried, he really tried, he fought his hardest.

As I'm trying to fall asleep, Lindsay taps me on the shoulder.

"Hey," she says. "I don't blame you. I wouldn't really want my mom here either."

"What are you saying?" Anna asks. "Of course they should be here. We can protect them."

"How would you protect them? Put our moms inside this glass box with us? Should they be naked too? Do you want them to bend into a saucer, a teapot?" Lindsay tries to stand up but bangs her head on the ceiling. Anna and I are sitting cross-legged at her feet. I look up and see the long curve of her spine.

"My mother might die because I didn't let her inside Worldly Wonders," I whisper to myself and to them. "But I don't think I regret it. I could never perform for her. She'd laugh, and then all of this would be ruined. I know it's selfish, but I just can't risk it."

The girls are silent for a while, and then Anna places her hand in mine and Lindsay does the same.

"I don't want to go home either. I feel in control here," Lindsay says. "I feel like a celebrity. The visitors care about me. They think I'm special. I know it's sad, but I don't think I've ever felt that way before."

"Do you think they still care about us?" Anna asks.

"I think so. I think they still love us. It's just coming out differently," Lindsay says.

"I hope that's not what love looks like," I say.

"Well, I hope it is," Lindsay snaps at me. "And what about that man from before? Do you think he loves you? Do you think he loves Anna and me? If you don't think it's love, why aren't you protecting us? Why aren't you protecting yourself?"

Lindsay turns away from Anna and me. She places her body as

far away from us as possible. I look at her back. Our paint is finally starting to come off. I rub the last bits of white off Lindsay's spine.

"I can watch you," I say after a few moments. "I can love you, and I can promise you that it'll be real. I can be your audience."

Lindsay looks back at me. She turns her body toward Anna and me. Anna places her thumb in her mouth and starts cleaning Lindsay until most of the paint is removed from her stomach.

"Me too," Anna says. "I will love you too."

I pull Lindsay's legs toward us. She topples over, and we lie like that—shapeless and touching. That night, we sleep stomach-to-spine. Our arms wrapped around one another tightly, like a rope pulling us closer and closer together.

In the middle of the night, Anna quietly asks me if I can give a tour, tell a story, just for them. A selfish story, she says. About only us, just for us.

"Once upon a time, in the land of China," I begin, "the girl with the dagger in her head was stolen by a nun and taught how to kill. When the nun finally gave the girl back to her parents, years later, they asked the girl what had happened. 'If I told you the truth, you wouldn't believe me.' 'Tell us anyway,' her parents implored. The girl with the dagger in her head told them how she was taken away to a cave. There were two girls there. They didn't eat and they could fly across the cliffs like gibbons. They were beautiful. The nun instructed her to learn from the girls, and soon the girl with the dagger in her head became as light as air and forgot her body too. In the first year, the girl with the dagger in her head learned how to cut off the heads of hawks and falcons. In the third year, of leopards and tigers. The nun told the girls exactly what to kill and how. She never gave a reason. With each death, the dagger in the girl's head became smaller and smaller. After each kill, the three girls placed the severed heads in a cloth pouch, and the nun transformed the heads into water. Every night the three girls walked to the garden and drank from the same pouch. They formed their palms into bowls. The water that dripped from their mouths fell softly onto the flowers. When they were together, the girls were never thirsty.

"After the girl had finished her tale, her parents stared at her in horror. Finally, her mother spoke. 'Why do I need to know this, Yin-niang?' her mother asked. The girl with the dagger in her head looked up. Usually, nobody called her by a name. She had almost forgotten what it was."

"Is it real? Are your stories real?" Lindsay asks. Her breath teases the back of my neck. I nod.

"Good. That's what I thought. It felt real," Anna says. The girls fall asleep quickly.

That night, I borrow a dream of Lindsay's for the first time. When I notice it is hers, I want to wake myself and quickly give it back. I see her as a young girl. She is inside her house, massaging her mother's back. Her mother is sighing with pleasure, telling Lindsay to press harder. Lindsay does as she's told. Her mother begins to scream, and I think it sounds like pain but I'm not sure. Underneath her screams, Lindsay's mother tells her daughter to press even harder. I watch Lindsay jab her thumbs into her mother's spine, and Lindsay starts to cry. I hear the door open, and it's Lindsay's father. He stands in the doorway and silently watches his wife and daughter. He listens to the sounds. When Lindsay finally looks at him, with tears in her eyes, her father simply walks back out the door. This is where the dream ends. I wake up and see Lindsay's and Anna's eyes wide and glistening. We let ourselves cry together.

From then on, the three of us start to exchange dreams.

At night, when nobody is watching, the girls and I start bending ourselves into a bowl again. We eat from one another. For a week, the girls and I save our meals and let them stack up inside the chute. In the dark, we can be our own audience. In the dark, we decide to feast. I lick noodles off Lindsay's spine. Anna cups soup in her hands and Lindsay sips the broth, clear and steaming. We grow sticky with one another's spit.

After a while, there's nowhere to dump our leftovers. The tubes are getting clogged, and it's been a week since someone has come to collect our trash. We leave our food scraps on the floor. We sleep on top of them. In my dreams, I often forget my own name. The three of us now have the same dreams almost every night—we are long, thorny roots at the bottom of a forest floor; we are the plastic swimming at the bottom of the ocean; we are the same son our parents always dreamed of having. I wonder what our names were before we had names. I wonder what my body was called when the world was preverbal, prewritten. I sink my spine farther into the floor. We bury our bodies in what we've eaten, what we've cut, what we've served to one another. We wait for everything to regrow, and we hope to grow along with it.

In the eighth week, the director announces that everyone must now relocate to China. It seems all of the countries in Worldly Wonders are infected now except ours. Thousands of visitors slowly march to China, their heads hanging low, faceless. Hundreds of people move their belongings into the room our box is in. They stare at us. Jealous. "Oh, to be in a glass box and safe. Oh, to be a beautiful Chinese girl. How flexible, how delicate. She must have been able to bend the virus from her body, contort it from her bones." Some visitors even ask the director if they can be in the glass with us. The director refuses. He says it's for their own protection.

After that, a visitor cuts off the water supply to our glass box. I think it's my will-be husband. I think he's mad at me. I'm almost certain he's trying to teach me a lesson. Soon Lindsay, Anna, and I grow in our stink. We become dirtier than the audience ever thought we could be. I kick the edge of the box, but it refuses to crack. Our soil fogs up the glass. I draw pictures in our stench. I write out my name. Not knowing what to do next, I draw a heart, a rainbow, a star. I feel stupid. Lindsay and Anna start drawing. They write their names too. Sam comes up to the glass and asks if there's anything he can do to help. He and Josh used to talk about rescuing me, but until now they'd stopped coming to the glass box. They'd been afraid of the visitors turning on them. Today when I ask about the possibility of escape, Sam tells me I'm probably safer in there. Nobody can touch me. Nobody can hurt me.

That night, while lying in our stench, Lindsay proposes that we paint one another. "Let's at least choose what we transform into." With my spit and the dried bits of food on the ground, I draw on

Lindsay and Anna. I remove their curves. I make them all edges. I ask us to come together, to combine, and I start painting myself. When I'm done, I look at us in the glass. I then try to see past our reflections into the darkness. I wish the audience could see us now. We are hard and crackling, sharp and stiff. "I wish we could stay like this forever," Anna says. "I wish we could always look like this."

My will-be husband must have changed his mind. He must have been able to smell us and felt sorry, because a day later our water supply is turned back on. In the morning, I hear our drinking tube rumble. I hold my hands underneath the tube, bring it to my mouth, and quickly swallow. My throat immediately starts to burn. I gag, and Lindsay and Anna wake up. Anna dips a finger into my cupped palms and smells it. The visitors have replaced the water with hand sanitizer. When we go to clean ourselves the next morning, the hand sanitizer burns our bodies, turning our skin rough. Everything smells sharp. I have to close my eyes tightly. I have to keep my mouth closed too. I try not to breathe.

That night, I ask the girls if we can sleep one on top of the other, a small, thin stack. They agree and I place myself at the bottom. Our breathing soon matches up. That night, I dream the beginning of our dream, Lindsay dreams the middle, and Anna dreams the end. We are a young girl swimming in a pool. Our father is floating, resting us against his stomach. Everything is silent. We don't know yet what water really is.

* * *

It's been three months of living in the glass box. People within Worldly Wonders China are now growing sick. Fewer people are watching our shows and more are lying down, coughing, spitting, spewing their uncleanliness throughout the room. It seems as if Anna, Lindsay, and I are the last healthy people. The park turned our water back on, but we've refused to clean our bodies. We make ourselves into a new naked. As the numbers dwindle, the audience grows angry. Angry that we've survived this long. Angry that we have caused this, that this thing has seeped into them but not into us. That somehow we've been immune to our stench. This is our greatest sin.

I learn that my will-be husband has made a request to the director. He wants to rescue me from the other girls. He wants me to be the lone Chinese girl in the glass box. After dinner, he comes up to the glass box with the director. My will-be husband wants us to fight. He wants me to hit Lindsay and Anna. The director is the one who tells us this. The director is in the pagoda for the first time, and he isn't leaving. My will-be husband has paid good money for this, and the director has to make sure that everything is seen through.

Lindsay and Anna get down on their knees. I stand up, my hand shaking. I extend my arm backward, swing it forward, and bring my palm just inches from the small of their backs. Lindsay and Anna hit the ground loudly with their fists, trying to imitate slapping noises. They close their eyes, their lips pressed tight. They try to scream but nothing comes out. Without warning, I hit their backs. Lindsay and Anna's mouths open in surprise, and I make sure my noise comes out of them. I scream for all of us. I look out toward the audience, and I hear them cheering. When I close my eyes, I think I can hear Caleb's voice, somewhere in the room, in the center of the crowd, hidden and deep. I scream even louder. I can almost hear what my audience is thinking: *What a strong Chinese girl on display. What a beauty. How frightening.* From the corner of my eye, I see the director watching me, his mouth open. I wonder if he's borrowing my noise too.

Once upon a time, in the land of China, the girl with the dagger in her head was given her final instruction to kill. It had been ten years since the girl had seen the nun. The nun told Yin-niang that she needed to kill at least one of the girls she had trained with. "Why?" the girl asked. "Why a human? Why them?" And just as always, the nun said nothing. For six nights, the girl with the dagger in her head traveled on the back of a paper donkey to the cave that lay next to a garden. There she found the two girls, as beautiful as ever, untouched and weightless. The three stared at one another and walked out to the garden together, hand in hand. The girl knew it was time to remove the dagger from her head. She laid her body on the garden ground, and in a single motion, removed the dagger. It sparkled brilliantly like a mirror. In its reflection, she saw only the two girls. They had never looked more beautiful. The girl with the dagger touched her head. Blood fell softly onto the flowers. The blood was so dark it looked almost blue. It only made the flowers want to grow more. Wordlessly, the two girls walked toward Yin-niang. They bent down and softly kissed her wound. They placed their fingers on either side of the wound and stretched it long and wide until it lay open before them like a window. On their hands and knees, they crawled inside it like babies. Immediately, the wound wrapped around them and closed. The girl with the dagger ran her fingers along the top of her head, and her body began to hum.

*   *   *

That night, I wake up Lindsay and Anna. They haven't moved since this afternoon. I think the audience believes they're dead. As soon as their eyes open, I start to record a history of the three of us. I draw our bodies on the walls of the glass box—with our spit, with our shit. I make a diagram. I color-code which parts of our bodies are silent, which parts of our bodies are loud. I locate the most Asian parts of ourselves and draw a careful diagram. I leave it up for the rest of the park, for some unknown people years or centuries later to read and to study, to learn about the Chinese girls who outlasted, who were dirty to their core, who stank and stank and stank.

I lie on the glass floor of the box and Lindsay and Anna do the same. The three of us transform. Our bodies now share a single memory. Something deep in our bones. We contort ourselves into the same shape without saying a word. We forget our names. We forget our friends and partners. We forget our mothers. We forget our past selves. We simply build ourselves into one another, lock our limbs, and wait until morning. As we sit in the barely-there sunlight, we start to grow. We breathe ourselves in, feel our bodies hum. We wait as the sun comes up. I smell us—wet, dark, and sharp. I glance at our reflections in the glass. I blink ourselves into view, and we're not something I recognize. The first visitors start to awaken. Together we open our mouths, and something comes out. We know exactly what it is.

EL SEÑOR
DE LA PALMA

by EDMUNDO PAZ SOLDÁN
translated by JENNA TANG

THE CHALANA DROPPED ME off on a dock next to a ship that transported machinery. As I swung my backpack onto my shoulder and disembarked, the captain told me to watch out: the cult of El Señor de La Palma had spread throughout the area, especially among the workers at the packing house and plantation. I told him not to worry, that all I wanted was to get out of the city for a while. Of course, I didn't tell him my reasons. I felt a cold wind against my chest, a discouragement.

They were unloading boxes in the warehouse when I got there; I took a piss next to a trash can blossoming with rotten bananas. A young man told me I was on private property and to clear out or he'd set the dogs on me. I told him I was a new hire and showed him my contract. He took a list of names out of his pocket and looked it over. Then he made me sign a paper and pointed out the way.

"It'll take about twenty minutes. It's swampy. I hope you brought some protection. The mosquitoes here are relentless."

At least it had stopped raining.

The employees' rooms at the packing house were filthy rabbit hutches that measured two meters by five. There must have been about eighty rooms, side by side, framing a rectangle around a concrete soccer field. Some had their windows open, allowing glimpses of beds, kitchenettes or mini gas stoves, and clothes stacked against the wall; boxes of detergent, bottles of soda, and dolls with eyes like tunnels to the end of the world were balanced on planks disguised as shelves. Each room had a number painted on the wall out in the hallway; I was assigned to twenty-nine.

I was exhausted and my pants were muddy from the walk; the humidity was stifling and the air was a solid mass. A boy with a runny nose leaned out of the window next door as I was about to enter my room and asked if I wanted to see his fish. Before I could answer, he pulled a catfish out of a bucket of brown water. He wanted me to hold it, but I refused. His mother pulled him back inside and scolded him.

The employee residential area was surrounded by irrigation and drainage canals. Beyond the canals, among the palm trees, you could see ice floating in the pools where the bananas were cooled, the warehouse where they were packed, and the path that led to the plantation. Through the warehouse window, a group of gloved workers toiled with their mouths covered by face masks and their cheeks swollen with coca. I wanted to lose myself in a job like this, to learn my lesson once and for all.

A picture with a brass frame welcomed me at the warehouse entrance, right next to a satellite antenna; in it was a drawing of an Indigenous person wearing an astronaut's helmet, and buckled into a seat attached to a rocket trailing smoke. Below it, I read the words PRAYER FOR EL SEÑOR DE LA PALMA.

The foreman, a fat man with a machete at his waist, extended his hand to me without taking off his gloves. He introduced himself as Rosendo and called Luisa over with a whistle. She was skinnier than the last time I'd seen her but was just as bubbly as always. She'd dyed her hair and the tips were gleaming, so blond they were white. She wore a pair of ill-fitting red heels and a tight dress. I thanked her for the opportunity.

"That's what friends are for. When I heard about your troubles, I didn't give it a second thought. Keep your head down and work hard for a few weeks and I'll make sure you get promoted. This place is isolated. No one will bother you here."

"I'll manage with whatever you give me. If you want, I'll tell you the whole story."

"There's no need. El Señor de La Palma is here for moments like this."

Rosendo explained what to do. The bunches came in from the plantations on cableways. They were unloaded onto banana rollers, where the bunches were sorted by quality, then placed in boxes. The workers finished at six. Dinner was served at seven, and then they were allowed to return to their rooms and were expected to be ready at six the next morning. It was around twelve hours of work, when the contract specified eight. I decided not to say anything. All I wanted was to lose the people who were looking for me in Cochabamba.

As soon as the clock struck six, the workers took off their masks and started shouting at one another in excitement while checking their phones. Almost all of them broke into applause. Luisa took me outside and explained the secret of this place: Don Waltiño, the owner of El Señor de La Palma plantation and packing house, had convinced his workers to invest their daily wages in the purchase and sale of a virtual currency that he had created and baptized as the Bitllete. The currency never stopped increasing in value; at the rate it was going, you could triple your investment in seventy days.

"I already have ten thousand dollars. When I reach thirty, I'll leave. It's a sure bet, especially for us promoters who work with Don Waltiño. That's what you should aim for."

"I don't know, Luisa. I'm not interested in easy money. I just want to disconnect for a while. I'm more than happy with shelter and something to eat for a couple of weeks."

"It's not easy money, Valentín. You'll see."

Around the soccer field, near the dorms and the kiosk, the workers were mesmerized by their phones: screens lit up in the semidarkness, digital flames in the jungle. Every second, an app updated the results of the investments with sounds and notifications: alarms, bells, signals. They didn't receive daily wages; everything was converted into digital currency.

"And they can't pay me in cash? I need the money. I only have a hundred bolivianos left, and I'm drowning in debt. I spent the last of my savings to get here."

Luisa's nostrils flared, as if she smelled a strange animal.

"Don Waltiño wants us all to be entrepreneurs willing to take risks with investment. He doesn't accept those who are satisfied with their low wages. Your contract is for a month, right? If you still feel like this isn't your thing after two weeks, then you can leave. But you'll want to stay for sure. The rumors say nobody can leave this place, but it's actually the other way around. So many applicants have to be chased away. We'll pay you ten Bitlletes a day."

Luisa's faith was contagious. I'd given up on quick fixes—something had gone wrong every time I'd tried to take a shortcut—but I didn't have the energy to argue with her.

I thought about sending my mom a text message when I got back to my room, but I didn't do that, either.

That night, Luisa gave me a tour of her little house. It was full of luxuries: she had her own bathroom, a living room and a kitchen, and good mosquito netting on her windows. Company posters lined the walls, and on a table was a pile of folders, pencil cases, and notebooks emblazoned with Don Waltiño's ruddy face. Many things were said about him: that he was a model of professional success born in a village near Chimoré; that, according to legend, at the height of his power he had slapped the president in the face for raising taxes on the export of edible products to Argentina. You wouldn't give him a second glance when you saw how chubby, short, and double-chinned he was, but he had come to own five hundred hectares of plantations in Chapare and to export a million cases of bananas per year. Then came the pressure from the government, which led him to close the packing house and sell off a good part of his properties. Some said he fled to Miami, others said he went to Buenos Aires or San Pablo. He came back a while ago with a pretentious new name for the company—El Señor de La Palma—and a project that attracted many families in the region, who offered up their savings to become part of it.

"I get a commission for each worker I sign up," said Luisa. "Not bad, but that's not as important as the other part. The philosophy. Because it's a life philosophy. It changed my life and I hope it changes yours as well. Don Waltiño is amazing. He supports me and takes great care of me. I seized the opportunity he gave me, and here I am, part of the *biz*."

"Out there, people think it's a cult. A religion."

"It's everything at once, Valentín. We want people to develop. When they get into the world of business, they help their families and the community. Individual drive and personal branding are very important. Once you get the hang of it, you'll love it."

She helped me set up my employee account. Given my situation, I didn't want her to have my email address or personal information; she explained to me that all transactions on the company's app were encrypted and that there was no security issue. Anyway, she accepted my false name and information. With that name I could exchange my electronic currency for real money.

"*Personal branding*," I repeated as I left. People say the craziest things.

After dinner, I lay down on my cot. I was so tired that not even the mosquitoes bothered me anymore, and before long I was snoring. The noise of a plane woke me up around four in the morning. They fumigated in the dark.

I couldn't go back to sleep. Luisa's face and those of the workers staring at their phones kept coming back to me.

I checked the Cochabamba newspapers, surprised by the speed of the internet connection. They talked about the bankrupted real estate development company, about a deal in Pacata Alta and the employees who had gone on the run. Not much else was known. I saw my name.

When all hell broke loose, I had thought about turning myself in to the police, explaining that I was just the one who showed the land to interested parties and didn't know anything about how my bosses handled things. A friend made me see that the angry mob wouldn't care about logic. Besides, hadn't I lived well all those months, thanks to the commissions? Nothing but expensive whiskey and brothels.

I went out to look for a toilet, and the humidity hit me. The mosquitoes had painted welts on my legs. The stars were breathing. A bat fluttered near my head, a dog barked furiously when I turned on the flashlight.

I went back to my room. My neighbor was crying.

Oh, Luisa. She hadn't changed a bit. She was just as fast when I met her in college. That was why she hadn't been able to stand the local pace and left for Brazil before the end of her second semester. I thought about our destinies, so different or maybe not, because in the end I didn't accept living on a small salary, either.

I had to get out of here as soon as I could. Two weeks, I promised myself. I'd act like I was interested so Luisa would leave me alone, but I'd stick to my original plan of going to Santa Cruz.

I opened the app on my phone. In My Account, the zero pulsed on the screen, huge and yellow.

* * *

My first shift was in the morning, after breakfast. The bunches arrived on cableways covered in plastic; I removed the stained bananas, fumigated the remaining ones, and left them on the banana rollers for another worker to box. A mechanical job that made me drowsy and gave me the feeling that I was on this planet for the sole purpose of making those movements. I surrendered vehemently to that truth. I had to quiet my aspirations.

I spoke with Rosendo and told him that the contract said eight hours a day, as the law indicated. He told me to complain to Don Waltiño.

"And when is he coming?"

"You'll see him very soon, one way or another."

In the afternoon, I found myself counting the minutes till six o'clock. I closed my eyes and saw a gleam in the warehouse, an aura around the bananas. Perhaps the glow of the jungle was filtering through the packing house. Or maybe it was just me, always so impressionable.

I checked my phone at six. I didn't have ten Bitlletes but twelve.

The woman from the room next to mine came up to me to show me how many Bitlletes she'd earned. Rita came from a nearby Ayoreo community. Her husband had gone to work on the coca plantations. She had saved up a good amount working at the packing house, but not having the money in her hands made her nervous, she told me.

"Me too," I said. "Maybe if we get some other people to join us, we could go complain and get paid in cash."

"Ay, I don't know." She swatted at her forehead, scaring off a mosquito. "I really respect Don Waltiño."

"One thing doesn't rule out the other. I think Luisa would listen to us."

"It's not just that. If it were only about money, it would be different. This is like a big family—you just have to get used to it. And my husband, I haven't heard from him for months."

She had signed a one-year contract and could only cash in her Bitlletes at the end. Still, she wasn't sure if she'd leave when her term was up. Her community was disappearing; some people had gone to the cities, others to the coca fields. This was her home now. She and her son had shelter and food. She frowned as if she regretted having these doubts, like she was afraid she'd been heard.

I would've loved to have had Rita's faith in El Señor de La Palma.

At least I had twelve Bitlletes in my account.

I thought about spending that first Sunday in Puerto Villarroel or Ivirgarzama, but Luisa told us we had a surprise waiting for us after lunch, and it was better if I stayed. Nobody left the company grounds. Some even went to work in the packing house and on the plantation in the morning.

Around three o'clock, people began to gather around the soccer field. The workers chatted and laughed. Rita was with her son, who clutched her skirt like she was going to escape. I put my hand on the boy's head and tousled his hair. The kid told me he could sell me a catfish. I said sure, and that I'd owe him for it. "Then no," he said.

The sun was scorching and I looked for a patch of shade. The branches of a tree above my head changed shape; I heard screeches and imagined a couple of playful monkeys among the leaves. A mountain pig grunted in the distance.

Luisa and Pedro approached an archway. She was holding a silvery metal projector in one hand, and he was carrying a stool; Luisa placed the projector on the stool and turned it on. Right away, a hologram of Don Waltiño appeared in the middle of the soccer field. It was my size and emitted a sunset glow that trembled occasionally, as if he was unsure of his presence and was trying to disappear. There were screams and applause.

"Welcome, Don Waltiño," said Luisa after asking for silence. "Thank you so much for your visit."

"Becoming an entrepreneur is great," Don Waltiño said in a booming voice that didn't come from his lips but seemed to radiate from every corner of the soccer field, as if it were God's hammer. "You have to think big, that's what El Señor de La Palma does. I started at the bottom, packing three boxes of bananas and traveling to Villazón in search of buyers. It's the only way out of poverty— work and generate wealth."

"We're all doing that here, Don Waltiño. Working hard from sunrise to sunset."

"Don't forget that I'm one of you. Bananas are in my blood. My first memories are of bananas and trucks. My parents lived in the upper valley, growing potatoes and raising sheep, and in the winter they came to Chapare to pick bananas and oranges to sell in Punata. I know that with just bananas, it can take a long time to accomplish what I have. That's why I've created this system of investment."

"We're all very pleased, Don Waltiño, watching our money grow by the minute."

"I just want to give you a starting point. In a few months you'll leave with your capital to invest in other businesses and others will step in here. You'll work hard and it'll pay off."

Don Waltiño pretended to observe us carefully as he moved from left to right. He spoke for about ten minutes, short sentences like something out of fortune cookies, easy-to-memorize phrases, until suddenly he said:

"Don't forget that I'm one of you. Bananas are in my blood. My first memories are of bananas and trucks..."

Luisa pressed a button on the projector and Don Waltiño disappeared. A roar of joy spread through the packing house. I congratulated her on putting together such a great show.

"I didn't like the mistake at the end. It doesn't usually happen."

I accompanied her to store the projector in a warehouse.

I checked the app on Monday night. After three days of work, I should have had thirty Bitlletes, but the total had reached forty-one.

I wanted to get El Señor de La Palma out of my head, but I couldn't. Living in the packing house meant working the day shift and then checking your phone until bedtime. The company's app also had games like blackjack and virtual slot machines where we could use our Bitlletes: a closed system for spending everything we earned. Rita told me her son had lost her a lot of money in those games.

Sometimes I nodded off with the phone in my hand.

In the evenings, I'd meet up with some workers to play cards near the kiosk. Doña Nancy, who ran the place, provided us with soda, matches, cookies, insect repellent, coca, and toilet paper. Women fanned themselves to shoo away mosquitoes, children played around the irrigation canal.

The next Sunday afternoon, we gathered around the soccer field again to see Don Waltiño. On Luisa's birthday, days later, the hologram of her favorite band, Maná, appeared. It occurred to me that you couldn't escape listening to Maná, not even in hell.

I shuffled the cards while chewing coca.

A few days later, Rita showed me news on the internet about a digital-currency scam in La Paz. "We aren't getting ourselves into trouble, are we?" she asked. I told her I'd talk to Luisa. Offended, Luisa responded that Don Waltiño was a respected businessman. I used those very words to calm my neighbor.

It would be ironic, I thought, to get a taste of my own medicine. I consoled myself by saying that at least I hadn't invested anything.

I dreamed of Don Waltiño. He seemed more real in my dreams.

Two weeks passed. I didn't enjoy the work or isolation, but money was piling up in the app. If Luisa's projections didn't fail, by the end of the year I would have the money not just to cover my debts, but even to keep some extra savings. I'd never wanted anything like that, but I wasn't stupid enough to put up a fight.

It was four months until December. I decided to wait until then to make up my mind.

One night, Luisa invited me to her house. She wanted to show me something. Exhausted after a long day in front of the banana rollers, I wanted to postpone the visit to the next day, but I saw how excited she was and didn't dare.

She greeted me with the curtains drawn and the room in semi-darkness. A young man busied himself next to the sofa, connecting a projector that rested on a round table. He was the technician in charge of the company's digital propaganda, come to show the new invention. "An upgrade," he said. I sat down on the couch.

The technician turned on the projector and Don Waltiño appeared. He was more intimidating up close; his amber glow made me blink. He moved around the room as though he recognized the place and stopped half a meter away from me; he held my gaze so intently that I ended up looking away.

"Good evening, Luisa," said Don Waltiño. "Good evening, Valentín."

"Good evening, Don Waltiño," I replied, forgetting that there would be no response from him, at least not a spontaneous one.

"I'm glad you're here," said Don Waltiño.

The voice surprised me from behind, brushed against me from the ceiling, ambushed me from the front: he was everywhere and nowhere. I clung to the sofa as if I were riding a bus with a cliff on one side, and the driver had accelerated.

"Entrepreneurship is the language of our time. Investment is the best way to build a better future."

The three-dimensional figure wavered and nearly vanished, blurring as if it were made of onion layers and had lost some of them.

He asserted himself again, even though he was somewhat pixelated.

"Growth is unlimited. We can compete with anyone."

Don Waltiño walked away from me. Now he was looking at Luisa.

"We have to believe in local talent. To get out of poverty, you have to work and invest."

"Here comes the best part," said the technician. "Luisa, get closer to Don Waltiño."

Luisa did as she was told. Don Waltiño grabbed her hands, as if he were about to dance with her. We could hear the sounds of a waltz. Luisa danced with him for a couple of minutes, the two of them synchronized, rhythmic, as if they'd practiced.

"It was so strange," Luisa said excitely as she sat down, "but also so natural. He's not a real person, but it was like dancing with one... I could feel him squeeze my hands. I even thought he was flirting with me."

"Now it's your turn." The technician signaled to me.

"Oh, I don't know. These kinds of toys aren't for me. I don't even dance with women."

"What you see here is not a man. Relax."

Don Waltiño extended his hand to me. I felt pricks on my palms, an itch that spread through my whole body.

"Give me a hug, Valentín," said Don Waltiño.

I did as I was told, thinking he would disintegrate in my arms. This wasn't a body, not entirely, but you couldn't call it a mirage either; it was like hugging a gelatinous substance. A substance that conducted currents and transmitted heat, emotions.

We danced awkwardly for a few minutes. I was sweating.

"Valentín, Luisa, you know the drill: innovate, innovate!" Don

Waltiño said as we parted, waving a hand as if he were greeting the public. "Good night, have a good night."

Don Waltiño froze with a sneer of surprise on his face. I asked the technician to turn off the projector. The figure disappeared.

"People are getting tired of the still hologram," said the technician. "We're experimenting with one that can interact with the public. The original gringo version is very expensive. We pirated like crazy and got a little creative here and there."

"Very convincing," I said. "So much so, it's scary."

"Don't be scared." Luisa smiled. "Don Waltiño is a teddy bear in any version."

"For now, he's able to hold basic conversations," said the technician. "We'll program more variation in his responses. The same goes with gestures, movements. We want to make him more fat-cheeked, chubbier, a little taller, which projects a sense of authority. These are powerful algorithms. They can do a lot."

"That would be amazing," said Luisa.

"Of course. El Señor de La Palma will be with us for a while."

I got up from the sofa and said goodbye to both of them.

During the week, it occurred to me that Don Waltiño might not exist at all. After my encounter with his hologram, I'd been searching the web and couldn't find any interviews with him. Or, I thought, maybe he did exist but hadn't returned to the country because he was frightened of the government, and a hologram had replaced him. Or perhaps a company he had nothing to do with was taking advantage of the fact that he'd become a symbol of success and was using his image without his consent.

I gathered my courage and called a cousin, who suggested I go back to Cochabamba to face the accusations.

I dreamed that Luisa was a hologram, and that I was one too. I dreamed that the packing house was a hologram.

One Saturday afternoon, I showed up at Luisa's house. I waited for her to finish checking a program that had just come in for the projector and told her that more than a month had passed and I wanted to leave. She kept typing on her phone, as though she didn't hear me. She did it very quickly, a talent I didn't have.

"Don Waltiño isn't going to like this at all." Luisa crossed her arms over her chest, twisting a curl between her fingers. Her look made me back toward the door. I asked her, between stutters, to pay me the equivalent of my Bitlletes in cash. She refused.

"Luisa, you knew... We'd agreed..."

"El Señor de La Palma helped you out when you needed it." She stood and faced me. "You'll wander from job to job again. And the police... One call and that's it. Think it over. It's not just about you. It's about all of us. *About me.* I'm trying to be a better person. I can't be wrong about my contracts. Don Waltiño says you have to see the soul of each person to discover whether they want to succeed in life. And I saw you, Valentín. I saw you a long time ago."

I didn't want to argue. I left her standing there.

Rita was mashing plantains in her room to make masaco; her son was watching cartoons on an iPad. I told her I'd come to say goodbye and encouraged her to come with me. I warned her that things would end badly if she stayed. She asked me when I was leaving. "Right now."

"I'll think about it," she said.

As soon as I left her room, I saw her heading to Luisa's house.

Rosendo knocked on my door and threatened to set his dogs on me. Rita stared at the floor, standing by the window of her room. Her son threw a teddy bear at me.

Luisa tried to convince me to stay. Sometimes she was kind and promised me a bright future; at other times she threatened me. I didn't listen to her reasons. I packed my few belongings into my backpack. Rosendo yelled that I should leave everything clean and tidy, and threw a broom at me. Rita offered to help and I told her not to bother.

The barking of the dogs accompanied me a long way.

At the dock, I waited for a chalana headed toward Puerto Villarroel. Luisa sent me several text messages but I didn't reply. If my suspicions about the place were right, she wouldn't call the police.

I took a taxi to Ivirgarzama and then hopped on a bus to Santa Cruz with my very last hundred. I lost my signal for a long time, and when it came back, I tried logging into the company's app. I couldn't. I thought about all the Bitlletes I'd accumulated and how I'd just lost them.

An old movie starring El Santo kept me entertained for a while.

I considered the possibility of starting a new business pre-selling houses and lots. All it takes is a good slogan, an attractive image.

As we passed Buena Vista I managed to fall asleep. I dreamed that Rita's son was selling me piles of catfish and that I paid him in cash.

ONE MAN AND HIS ISLAND

by NIMMI GOWRINATHAN

FROM THE OUTSIDE, ONLY the tips of leaves that bleed green to yellow tease the contents of his garden to suspicious neighbors. Though geographically displaced, the peeking banana tree nestled in the far corner is his centerpiece. He is pleased that his secret garden stands out "like a sore thumb," as he says, refracting the gaze of passersby as envy of his innate talent for nurturing a green habitat in the desert.

He is proud, too, of the cascading fuchsia that lines the edges of the over-mortgaged property. In Tamil they were *kadathaasippoo*: tissue-thin paper flowers. The vowels of the English word borrowed from the French *bougainvillea* fall uncomfortably on his accented tongue. It is to this plot on the very edge of Los Angeles County that I have always returned.

Here, his fortress is the only creatively colored spot on a uniformly pristine street. Its other occupants are committed to their own land agenda: a diasporic enclave of orthodoxy dedicated to maintaining the territorial integrity of the state of Israel.

Banana trees dot the peripheries of childhood memories on the island. He doesn't speak about life "back home" very often—the land there was never his birthright. His grandfather fished the waters of the eastern shore, and when the rioting mobs reached his family, they took refuge in the tented camps on the northern peninsula. His family never owned land, and communal property would eventually be seized by the state. Displacement was the only inheritance for him and the one million other Tamils who were uprooted, scattered, forced to repopulate on hostile terrain.

He arrived in California via Oklahoma. The writer Carolina Miranda's remapping of the state reflected his own statelessness. "Before California was West," she writes, "it was North and it was East: the uppermost periphery of the Mexican Empire." Whenever news reaches him in Los Angeles of the endless war against his people in Sri Lanka, he shakes his head and says, "Stupid banana republic country…," unknowingly adopting the white condescension toward Central America. He does speak often (and passionately) of stolen homes in Palestine. The subject releases sublimated rage: a referred pain radiating West, settling in another landless body.

In his relentless pursuit of repossessing his own corner plot, he wanders around the nurseries of suburban America, where reddened white faces barely register his existence. He limps through rows of pots on a fickle hip. Once, I was trailing him in a sprawling warehouse when he stopped at a familiar spread of palm leaves artificially nurtured in a greenhouse. The owner glanced up from beneath the brim of his trucker's hat long enough to scoff. "If you're planting that here, no way it survives. Unless you're planning to take it to an island or something." He smiled and thanked the gentleman. Since his earliest days as an implant, he has feigned ignorance in the face of racist aggressions. Deploying charm to disarm malice is his own natural adaptation to survive in a new environment.

Here, he has never been terribly concerned with guidelines or stated rules. He asks me to climb nursery display cases to take down the largest hydrangeas, dismissing my protests. "This is America," he says. "We're free to do what we want."

He admires the foliage transplanted to other immigrant-refugee homes, their value inflated by illegal acquisition. The seeds of karuvepillai (curry leaves) were smuggled over borders in pill bottles; malligai poo (jasmine) was plucked stealthily from neatly mowed botanical gardens. The rules were trampled in service of a higher cause.

There is rarely a blueprint for these restored gardens. His own haphazard wilderness spills carelessly onto public sidewalks, leaving a trail of city citations at his front gate. Back home, guerilla fighters and besieged civilians alike desperately try to blend into the background, eluding the predatory eye of the surveillance state. Here, he is hyper-visible on his own terms.

Some days he wakes up early to make his way downtown to the Los Angeles Flower District, returning satisfied with his open trunk full of plants but unsettled by the sleeping bags strewn across San Pedro Street. To have land, an immovable home, should be every person's right in a country such as this.

He was born on the cusp of the island's independence from the shackles of imperial whiteness. A racist control turned inward, repurposed to hold his community captive. He left with no claim to the plates of earth converging into a state that sought to separate. In his own bid for freedom, he would avoid recruitment into the camouflaged rebel movement holding the line of self-determination in the jungle.

Here, his political beliefs do not immediately put his life at risk. Once, at a California fundraising event, he sauntered past the Secret Service to offer then president Bill Clinton his thoughts on addressing homelessness—scribbled on the back of a receipt for weed killer from Home Depot.

Back home, it was the wobbly legs of a water tank, the speckled trunks of jackfruit trees that marked family property. The bright hibiscus plants he pulls up the blinds to reveal every morning were naturally interwoven across neighborhood terraces on the island. A fluid but clear ecosystem of coexistence. Here, he—we—import memories in potted soil, constantly trying to affix permanence to land. There is a frenetic energy with which he adds more and more to his yard, nurturing the newcomers with extra water. "You have to make sure they are firmly rooted." A repetitive frame to conjure up his desired reality. Nonetheless, some days the anxiety of loss is so palpable that even the flourishing blossoms feel fleeting.

Dead land is vulnerable to colonization. "Just as cartographic emptiness invited settlement, it also created a space into which others could project their illusions," Miranda notes. Myths take hold before the invasion of heavy artillery of colonization: the native inhabitants attached to the soil are unskilled in its cultivation.

Plant-a-tree pamphlets urging residents to populate the forests of a Zionist imaginary encircle his home in Los Angeles as the imported Aleppo pines create a tinderbox in Palestine. Selective sciences (political, geological, social) are deployed to divide up the topography of the homelands slipping away from the dispossessed. The year the drought sapped his yard here, the dry zone back home was split into "safe" zones and military targets. An indiscriminate distinction: Tamil bodies fell equally across the divide.

In this, the final stages of a decades-long war in Sri Lanka, the vegetation of the homeland hardened against shelling from above and the cracking ground below. Evidence of the bloodshed decayed quickly as the arid soil buckled under the weight of battle tanks, legitimizing theft inside the new boundaries of land known only as "high-security" zones. If stories have two sides, theirs centered the joy of carefully splitting a ripened breadfruit; ours the pain harvested for outside consumption.

Back home, the palmyra was the giving tree for survival—resisting drought, deconstructing itself to offer leaves for shelter, fibers for rope. Two million palmyras had been shelled or stripped in the years since he left the island: bloodied beaches left pockmarked by their decapitated crowns.

Here, he concedes to the state ordinances aimed at preserving water on the outside—planting desert flowers on the strips of his land that line the street, visible to the public. On the inside, he continues to religiously water his miniature palms under cover of darkness.

On the island, he would buy strands of jasmine for his wife's hair from the street seller outside the temple walls. Here, he carefully combs his garden for the perfect roses to offer her altar room. For me, there is always one special bloom floating in a cup on my childhood dresser that welcomes me, back home.

If the settlers ever came to take his land, if he had to choose, my father would save his banana tree.

THE INJURY
by MJ BOND

BRUISING

IT'S STILL EARLY. I push blackberries against the roof of my mouth, slowly. The sun barely gives shadow in the kitchen. I feel the light through sheer green curtains, a dry lick across my back. The berries turn to liquid on my tongue. The ripe sweetness moves through my throat and chest and drips down to my stomach.

A friend overdosed and was in a coma for a week. Her face was bloated and pinkish, like a newborn's, and was held up with a stiff white neck brace. Her hair was matted with sweat and hung heavy around her ears and cheeks. I was told to pray for her, to think of her kindly.

I filled the first thin needle an eighth of the way with testosterone, rubbed the outer side of my thigh, and slowly pushed through my skin and into my muscle. I was drunk and didn't switch the syringe needle to the injection needle. It left a small yellow-and-green bruise. It was seven days after this that she overdosed, her body strapped to a hospital bed.

I was in New York. Faith swallowed the thousand-mile gap between us. She was alone when she overdosed—they tell me fentanyl.

Her family made the decision: the nurses pulled the cord. I got the call in the morning. I said, Okay. I moved myself to the bathroom, my mind pushing outward, beginning to melt on my skin. I filled the needle an eighth of the way and injected it into my thigh. I didn't cry for two days, then I filled the needle an eighth of the way and stuck it into my thigh again. Another two days, again, and again. A month of doses in a week; an imitation.

Paul B. Preciado writes:

> From this moment on, all of you are dead. Amelia, Hervé, Michel, Karen, Jackie, Teo, and You. Do I belong more to your world than I do to the world of the living? Isn't my politics yours; my house, my body, yours? Reincarnate yourselves in me, take over my body…

I told the first person about the death after the doses of testosterone made me feel like I was seductively coked-out. She asked if I needed anything, I said no. I waited for her to hang up first.

Months pass, two or so. In the kitchen, the morning light begins to reflect off the snow. It reaches the lower branches of the trees, it reaches into the kitchen. When I inhale, I wrap another blackberry with my tongue. On the exhale, I press the fruit against the back of my teeth.

When the breath comes in, it moves through my mouth to my esophagus, passes my tearing larynx and through my trachea, then disperses into my lungs through two bronchi.

The thyroid is above the trachea; it's shaped like a butterfly. Butterflies are thought to be the most notable form of after-death communication. I read this on a website, where the words "After-Death Communications Confirm That Life and Love Are Eternal" are displayed in a giant and nearly illegible cursive font. After the butterfly there's the trachea, which looks like a straight pipe that branches into the right and left bronchi.

When the trachea is inflamed, it doesn't become enlarged; its exterior remains the same size. It is the inner tissue that swells, creating a moderate-to-extreme narrowing of the airway. This makes it hard to take a deep breath. This also means you may have to chew your food enough that the swallowed substance is nearly liquefied.

Some common symptoms of tracheobronchitis are:
severe cough
a sore throat

fatigue
shortness of breath
wheezing
cyanosis.

Grief lives in my trachea. Time does not pass well. I breathe in counts of two and juice the blackberries in my mouth. I let them move through me, dewing the swelling with sweetness.

Inflammation is more likely to occur in the larynx, the voice box. The larynx is above the thyroid, close to the opening of the mouth. Its swelling can be visible in proper conditions: with access to hospital fluorescent lights and a decent camera. The inflammation turns the throat from a circular hole into a thin slit, and it feels constrictive. This case is more familiar.

My larynx is torn and growing, the vocal folds lengthening and thickening. This will eventually make my voice adopt a deeper tonality, after a period of synthetic croaks. My larynx is only centimeters above the swelling. When the juice moves past my vocal cords, I feel uneasy. They are gaining a new texture, a scrape.

Testosterone causes ossification, or a hardening of the cartilage, making the larynx less flexible. This can create a condition called "entrapped vocality," in which the voice sounds weak.

I use three fingers as a tongue depressor and slide them deep into the middle of my throat. I tilt my head back, eyes closed, and gently prod around. This is one way I tend to my grief. I want to feel the scrape. I am careful not to touch the butterfly.

My fingers are damp with saliva. I pull them apart slowly and watch the saliva form a small thread that falls back against my fingers. The wetness is tinted with mucus and a dark blue, I lick it off my fingers. I feel the scrape, I cannot hear the butterfly, and the swelling remains.

Testosterone: a synthetic hormone to be injected at .21 milliliters every week. Viscosity like thick motor oil. Not quite opaque, yellow-tinted. Manipulates and redefines the body. Increased sex drive, higher risk of addiction, increased hair, deepened voice; narrowed emotions.

Each time I pull the needle out of my thigh, I feel the swelling grow closer to the butterfly, closer to the scrape. I want to protect the swelling; I want it to rupture like a thunderclap. Permanently.

The other night, I fucked someone with my body and desire, now controlled by synthetics. When she grabbed my throat, I think she wanted my tongue and I let her push harder against the swelling. She told me to come inside her—come in me, come in me, come in me. Come in you? One hand closing my throat, the other with a death grip on my thigh.

In the kitchen, I slip my boxers off and walk to the bathroom. My thigh is yellowish, and green in the middle, where her hand was. Come in me.

The bruise is a prize for my drone attachments, for becoming half-mechanized, a reduction of being, for keeping the scrape unscathed with a quiet voice, for feeding the swelling with the come still clotted on my molars.

Years, months, or days pass without acknowledgment of where the present has gone, where the body is shrinking and growing, attached and detached. It fluctuates, it's specific: the space between my jawline and collarbone is slouched and collapsing; the space where my ribs round off, my sternum, aches against the compression. I want this to rupture, to snap.

I have become addicted to the injection process. I worship the growth, the swelling, the bruise of a new body. New and kept, dose by dose, in a constant state of becoming.

Being: condition, state, circumstance; presence, fact of existing; that which physically exists, a person, a thing.

Becoming: change from one state of existence to another; meet with, fall in with; arrive, approach, enter.

I allow the golden oil to offer a new sense of linearity, to become *my body, yours?* The growth will never exhaust itself.

Timothy Morton writes:

The threads of fate have tied our tongues.

Tongue twisters inclined towards nonsense.

Logic includes nonsense as long as it can tell the truth.

The logic of nonsense.

The needle skipped the groove of the present.

Into this dark forest you have already turned.

I take *present* to mean *for the last twelve thousand years*. A butterfly kiss of geological time.

INCISION

I am unwrapping my index finger in a room, my palm facing down. First I unwind the masking tape wrapped around stained cotton balls and wet Band-Aids. Then I peel off the white fuzz that sticks to the wound, is inside the wound. Blood flows from the middle of the finger and drips onto the floor, following a dried red path. In the room, one window is covered with trash bags, held taut with blue painters' tape, and a duvet cover is nailed over that.

The cut is along the middle phalanx, the first joint after the knuckle. Tendons run through this joint, connecting the muscle to the bone. Nerve tissue surrounds the tendons, working with them to allow movement: bending and pointing. The cut is a quarter inch long, hard to spot through the eager blood.

I practice bending my finger for days: my brain sends signals but my finger stays limp and bloated. I prod at it, trying to move it with my other hand. I regret this immediately, pain shooting down my throat, back up my spine, to the back of my head. The blood rushes out in higher volumes. All I know is to keep it elevated, so I walk around with one finger in the air, as if I'm about to say something, the other fingers curving into my palm.

Glass has a disordered molecular structure. When it shatters, it goes from one piece to ten, twenty, plus a hundred more microscopic ones. The lack of order means that even the tiniest amount of damage immediately becomes the glass's weak point; the shattering is unavoidable. In the breakage, thousands of incisions form along the edge of the glass, acting as blades. An arsenal of weapons, dehydrated and waiting, dismembered and hiding in my carpet.

There are white spots forming around the injury. The nail bed has turned a light blue with white streaks. The flesh between the joints is swollen and bruised.

> *Cyanosis refers to a bluish tint to the skin. It's usually caused by low oxygen levels in the red blood cells. When this occurs, the blood becomes a darker red, meaning more blue light is reflected, giving the skin a blue tint.*

The cleaning process helps only to sterilize the wound. When I unwrap my finger, the bleeding starts again, regressing the healing, restarting the process. I apply chemicals to it patiently, tending to it like it's alive, like it has its own body. The act of breaking glass, when there is the intention of breaking, is often a ritual of remembrance. In Jewish tradition, a bride and groom smash a glass at their wedding to remember the destruction of the temple of Jerusalem. The broken glass becomes a symbol for the pain and sorrow that must be held, even on the most joyous occasions. As this weight of sorrow is remembered, it is also the utmost symbol of gratitude for the history that has brought the bride and groom together.

Breaking a mirror, on the other hand, is commonly seen as bad luck. The superstition originated with the Romans, back when mirrors were made of volcanic glass: obsidian. Obsidian was thought to be a portal to both the underworld and the afterlife; one's image in the mirror was not a reflection but was, in fact, one's soul. Thus, the fracturing of a mirror resulted in the fracturing of the soul. The Romans also believed that one's life was renewed every seven years, and so a broken mirror leaves one with seven years of bad luck. After that time, one's body is renewed, along with one's soul.

Like glass, obsidian lacks internal order—when it is shattered, it fractures into pieces invisible to the eye. It is used to craft the sharpest and strongest blades, delicate and smooth, blindingly reflective. Prior to obsidian, or even in continuum with it, water was used as a sort of mirror, a source for reflections. A somewhat translucent pool of water reflects back your image, which is drawn about with the streaks of the current, turning your silhouette into a dancing outline. The myth of Narcissus hinges on this reflective power of water. Ovid writes:

> It's here that, weary from the heat, the chase,
> drawn by the beauty of the pool, the place,
> face down, Narcissus lies. But while he tries
> to quench one thirst, he feels another rise:
> he drinks, but he is stricken by the sight
> he sees—the image in the pool. He dreams upon
> a love that's bodiless: now he
> believes that what is but a shade must be a
> body.

A broken window can be a sign that there was evil in your house and the broken glass allowed it to exit. A serendipitous severing of the interior and exterior.

Your reflection can best be caught in a window at night. In a room with the lights on, you can look through the window and see only yourself. The room's lights do not pass through the window; instead, they reflect back, creating a faint, holographic version of yourself. When there's lightness on one side and darkness on the other, you become the meridian, seeking a reflection.

Breaking the reflection, the window, can mean, like the myth of Narcissus suggests, that you are too entrenched in vanity: that you spend too much time reflecting on your appearance and image, reducing all meaning to your physicality. Dreaming about breaking a window can be a sign that you are burdening yourself with someone else's problems; it's an indicator of a weak sense of self.

Wrapping the wound is tedious; the cut reacts tenfold to anything that touches it. Shooting pain, pulsing flesh, spilling blood. It re-creates its initial trauma without hesitation, preying on its own physical form, its own scarring and rebuilding.

window (n.) c. 1200, literally "wind eye," from Old Norse vindauga, *from* vindr, *"wind." Replaced Old English* eagpyrl, *literally "eye-hole," and* eagduru, *literally "eye-door."*

Windows can serve as a sort of shield around the looker, the voyeur. Through the shield, the world looks back at them. The window enables the voyeur's passiveness; it draws a barrier between them and the surrounding world. When it is broken, the transparency lies on the floor, allowing entrance, action, connection. The person inside is left doe-eyed, facing down hundreds of high beams, fluorescent and daring.

Reflections in glass are thought to be analogous to the body; the reality of one's appearance and demeanor can be fully trusted in the reflection. But this puts too much trust, too singular a truth, in the mirror, in the likeness reflected back at you. The desire to define the body by the reflection is condemned as soulless and vain.

The window carries a similarly structured symbolism, focusing on the interior and exterior. If one finds too much comfort in the interior, the exterior will ridicule it, and the shattering will break the barrier. It seems the "glass shield" is a prop of some psychological shyness: the interior space becomes the body, the window becomes the eyes, the person inside is the naive voyeur.

The exterior is generalized, personified into a disciplined pair of eyes staring back, waiting. The fracturing proves the voyeur to be closed inside the body, shut behind the eyes—"closed mind," closed body.

Both window and mirror are reduced to the reflections in their glass: one looking at and one looking back. Neither of them should be held in differing esteems, or held in vain. The glass inevitably breaks, breaks again, breaks infinitely.

Ovid continues:

If I could just be split from my own body!

The strangest longing in a lover: I
want that which I desire to stand apart
from my own self. My sorrow saps my force;
the time allotted me has been cut short;
I die in my youth's prime, but death is not
a weight; with death my pain will end, and yet
I'd have my love live past my death. Instead,
we two will die together in one breath.

Narcissus dies in his own image, in love with his own image. He was unable, and did not want, to find love in others. Even the one who pursued him prior to reaching the pool of water, Echo, was not deemed worthy of his love.

Echo lives with a curse that allows her only to repeat what people say to her; she can never initiate speech, for herself or with others. When she sees Narcissus, she falls madly in love and follows him through the forest. She eventually jumps on him, trying to express her new and burning affection. Narcissus says, "Do not touch me! Don't cling to me! I'd sooner die than say I'm yours!," to which she fatefully repeats, "I'm yours."

Echo, in her brief moments with Narcissus, is an auditory mirror for his speech, an imitation. But this is not the reflection worthy of his love. It is in the steadfast image of himself, in still water, that he lays himself bare, accepting death. He dies by the side of his true love: his physical body, his exteriority. The duality in this myth is not vanity and selflessness, but the love of tongue and flesh.

Echo returns to the mountains, where her flesh disintegrates and her bones turn to stone. She remains as an echo: a resounding cry of grief that sounds through the caves and the land. "The power of sound still lives in her."

I buy a cast for my finger. It has a blue Styrofoam cushion surrounded by aluminum, *a bluish tint to the skin*, and two thin Velcro straps wrap around the finger to keep it stable and straight. This way, the nerve tissue, in case it's torn, will have a chance to reconnect and will heal within a month or so.

I begin to tell people that windows have souls, are the eyes of themselves, that the window is the soul of the eye, the soul of the window is not for the eye but of the eye, the eye's soul is the window is the soul.

I sleep through the morning sun. The room is congested with caught wind and dust; candle smoke is trapped, voices are trapped, smells are trapped. The dust begins to catch in my throat, becomes in my throat. My voice rasps in the mornings, I cough into tissues that pile around my bed. Entrapped vocality, making the voice sound weak and hoarse.

When I take off the duvet cover and trash bags, the sun greedily climbs through the window. It's instantaneous, unhesitating: a tsunami of light reaches around my body and paints everything with highlights and shadows. I turn the ceiling fan on, open the rest of the windows, and leave the room for a day. What was trapped will find an exit, and eventually I'll be able to speak through a sentence.

At night, I cover the window again.

Microscopic fragments still live in the carpet. There are a few shards left in the pane. I look at them from the outside, running my finger over them, trying to find matching textures. The shards are turned opaque by the darkness of the tightly taped trash bag. It's a cartoon-ish depiction of obsidian. It reflects my belt and jeans, the paint streaks across the pockets.

The fractures of the glass distort the reflection, the thin plastic bag in the middle sounds against the rushing wind. I lift my finger to reflect in one of the shards. I hold it slanted so the bottom of my hand, the space below the injury, casts shadows on the peeling white paint around the glass. The top of my finger reflects back to me in the smallest shard, reduced to colorlessness, a shadowed and saturated outline, a silhouette.

An imitation.

I compress my finger tightly in the cast. I use it to assist in vocal practices meant for loosening up the throat, healing the voice. An exercise called "the larynx ladder." I let out a groan in a high octave and place my wrapped finger under my jaw, where it connects to my neck. The cold aluminum is the only way I can tell it's on the right spot. I have to press hard against my skin, to feel for my larynx, hard and circular, vibrating above the aluminum. As I drop octaves (going down "the ladder"), I move the cast down my neck; it's pushed deep into the skin to mimic a spotter for the larynx. When moving from low to high notes, I place more of the cold pressure under the larynx, ushering it back to the high spot under my jaw.

I close my eyes during the practice, familiarizing myself with the brute and hoarse sounds. The high notes sound synthetic, as if coming from a helium balloon. The low notes are worse, monotone and flat. I can't find the sweet spot; the cold aluminum against my neck moves up and down the middle section, searching for a casual voice. What my voice is, naturally (now).

Narcissus is the bench player in his own myth. His idolization of himself, of his physicality, is just a deal with death, but Echo's voice lives on. The flesh has always been known to collapse. But the voice? The sound? She is the auditory mirror, stuck in her own grief, on the last consonant or vowel. Even if the word is another's, it is her sound; it is Echo with no body, her eternal song.

Someone comes to replace the window. He carelessly feels around the pane, then sporadically punches the glass that remains. I am in the neighboring room, gently poking my neck with the metal finger. I haven't taken it off for days; I've grown fond of the metallic reflections and distortions of light. He calls me in when it's finished and tells me the windows are at least a hundred years old, bound to break at any time. Old age.

My finger heals before I realize I can bend it again. By that time I have bought new curtains for all the windows in the house. I continue to let time suffocate in my room until it feels right; then

I pull back the curtains and watch the light dance manically into the room, swallow the space. The dust reaches high to the ceiling, and falls back, the sun illuminates its cycle.

AIN'T THEM BODIES SAINTS

by C. T. Mexica

A child is a lonely thing to put in prison
Without a lover lonely in its parent's care.
—Olga Broumas, *Perpetua*

SOME VATO, IN SOME pinta somewhere, must have unhooped his pedazo and noticed that it looked very much like a chocolate bar, except this Whatchamacallit was hard and hazardous, giving birth to another convict term of art: hard candy. Graveyard humor for the brutal intimacy of a shank reserved for the unwanted of the underworld. And also for enemies both made and inherited. Or for those once considered friends who were now ostracized. Removals and regime change were just part of the ruthless pragmatism of the demimonde. Private codes for a private world.

He had two pedazos in this situation. His captors knew that biology cannot be denied, and he'd eventually have to extract whatever he had hooped. The authorities were hoping the evacuation would produce any pedazo, clavo, or huilas that he'd gangstered up there. That is how he ended up in that dry cell. The toilet in a dry cell is essentially a toilet atop a fish tank, designed to recover any contraband inserted or ingested. In the private language of the imprisoned, inserting has evolved from keistering to hooping and gangstering.

For hygienic purposes, he had already trained himself to handle his business first thing in the morning. He'd seen men bludgeoned for farting among bona fide convicts. Same goes for those picking their Paris Hiltons. He liked to be light and clean, so he evacuated both his dookshoot and snotlocker way before breakfast was served. All shit, showered, shaved, and shined for the morning slop.

A snitch's accusation landed him and a few others in dry cells, and, as he was known to always be armed, the staff were waiting for him to evacuate whatever he had. And he would, but by then he had gotten into the habit of carrying two pedazos *in* his person. He'd give them their treat and keep the other. He still had a few hours to go until dawn, his self-trained routine, so he went about situating himself in that cold, bare cell and ignored the staff member sitting on the other side of the cell's observation window. As he became institutionalized, he began to appreciate the clarity of an austere cell. It reminded him that his courage must remain constant and that he must never abandon himself. He had long ago come to see punishment as a painful honor for bringing his enemies sorrow.

In those dry cells, he always thought of water, especially the flow of a river beginning in the floating lakes that nourished the rocky peaks of a high wilderness. Like his ancestors, he and his family were always on the move. The ancients followed the weather and were guided by mountains, all the while weaving their humanity into the cosmos of two continents. Over thousands of years, they filled those immense landscapes with vast localisms anchored in their dreamscapes.

His family eventually found a brave and grand river that became the special country of their hearts. His father's people would find themselves on the upper reaches of the grand river, where plateau cities abounded. His mother's people would find themselves in the sultry sea plain of the lower reaches of the brave river, where it freed itself from its long journey into a large basin of murky salt water.

Though once it was a brave and grand river that ran free and wild, now it was drowned by the acceleration of newcomers with lustful spirits. The newcomers blocked the river with barricades and boundaries. On the upper reaches, this hastening cultivated mutiny in the hearts of many who were eventually confined on reserves. Later, many of their children would be sent to schools where the dreams of their ancestors were either quieted or extinguished in the name of acceleration. His father told him that those children and all Indigenous children that followed were born prisoners of war. These confinements caused many to die of broken hearts. The lower reaches would be just as contested and would come to have men with guns on both sides, with families seeking relief from the cruelties of its lower bank. These families were halted and separated, and many of the children were put into cages in camps of saints bereft of tender mercies. Some of the unbroken among them would later find themselves in dry cells con sólo la melancolía de ese río.

In time, he came to think of it as a river with two kinds of pain. One was a steady, malevolent pain that felt like an abyss—an energy vampire feeding on an open wound. The other had a bridge that could quiet some of the pain of a journey where the way was long and the roads were bad.

His mother's gente were from inland South Texas, and he grew up running through that caliche dirt and brush country all the way up to the vaporous waters on the coast. When he was a child, he would listen to his elders talk in low, gentle voices about violent things. "What they did to us," some would say, "let their god repay." They talked about obras desalmadas and other evils visited upon their gente and against the land. One of the most recent cycles they called "the Hora de Sangre," on account of countless attacks and lynchings on real American dirt where periwinkles bloom.

His father's gente did not fare any better among the chamiso and piñon pine of northern New Mexico. They were last in Arroyo Hondo, home of a failed populist insurrection against another wave of expeditioners, who spoke a florid language that the locals would soon make their own. His father, like he, was state-raised in glad-iator schools. The son knew his father mostly through jailhouse letters. His father wrote in a fine longhand that the son emulated and that was once praised by a sweetheart as sinisterly elegant. She said it must have been the way Dracula wrote.

He was a prison baby whose institutionalization began in the maximum-security visiting room where his parents first met. That was his father's house. Long before he ever set foot in a detention center, he grew up in the prison cultures that the men, and later the women, brought home. When he was just a child, he could already hear tractors paving new routes to new prisons. Small-walled villages where criminal children came of age. Places where dreams were extracted and extinguished while childhood hid its departure from them. Places for good boys who did some awful things to bad people and bad boys who did awful things to one another. Boys who couldn't always hold the dark and came up in cells that gave their pain the dignity of privacy. The things many of them felt, they would rather have felt alone. Because much of life hurt, their fun included a lot of hurting. For every joy there were a hundred pains.

At the first detention center he was sent to, the juveniles were lined up in front of their cells before getting locked in for the night. This was the nightly ritual in which they removed their elastic-waisted tramos and canvas kicks and placed them outside their cell doors. The Bob Barkers were color-coded by waist size: green for the pip-squeaks, blue for the moderately inclined, and khaki for waves of confidence. The slip-on shoes were called winos by the boys with oblique eyes and high cheekbones. The boys with skin that don't crack called them croaker sacks. Some were there only in passing. Those were the juvenile delinquents. A smaller group was becoming impervious to the deprivations of incarceration. They were training themselves to endure hardships without complaint. Those were the true believers, who earnestly began their criminal apprenticeships. Children of adversity whose paper trails led to the joint, the criminal children who never intended to know any life other than that of banditry. They would grow up taking pictures in prison yards where they archived albums of outlawry. Those were the young convicts—a term of honor distinct from *inmate*. They inherited the convict code and adapted it for their generational circumstances, then passed it on to the next wave of true believers. No matter the variations, it would always be based on three prohibitions: no snitches, no rapos, and no chesters. Wherever bona fide convicts are warehoused, they will not program with those undesirables. Puros vatos felones who were honor-bound to create brave spaces for themselves wherever they landed.

His age group was the inaugural generation of mass incarceration. Their class years ranged from the late '80s to the early '90s. Some of them would skip grades and go straight into institutions of higher punishment. But first there were the gladiator schools. No graduation robes, just jumpsuits of varying colors. When he was seventeen, his high school diploma was unceremoniously slid under his solitary cell door, and he placed it on top of a neat stack of official paperwork until it disappeared in one of many cell searches. Ni modo. It be's that way sometimes, bro. The peer reviews he valued came from righteous convicts who let others know of his stellar underworld credentials. His reputation got to each facility long before he did.

When he was first sent to the institutions, he quickly learned that incarceration is more about what you have to become than what you want to be. That becoming was the emotional numbness on the face of an expressionless convict. It was unbecoming of the song his mother put into his heart. It was a gaze that prepared him for the tragedies to come. A resting face fed by prison's slow drip of adrenaline. He did it because he had to, then because he liked it and became good at it, and one day he came to believe he was meant for it.

What he had wasn't new. He first sensed it in the older men he grew up around. The men in his family were only unquestionably together in prison and in war. It was only in violence that they were ever truly refined and resourceful. Some of the older ones were sent to Vietnam to "win hearts and minds," but what they really did was steal the dreams of people who had never disturbed their peace. Those irreclaimable acts would haunt their sleep long after that war was forgotten at home. A war they brought home to their loved ones. And, after they returned, many of their sons became undone in prisons and later in deserts and mountain ranges that were worlds away. Invisible wounds festered and became a terror to the loved ones they would not let in, or to those they pushed away.

He would often think of these afflictions whenever he went back to the basics of a dry cell. But that night, he heard something other than his thoughts and memories. First, it was the sound of death, which he immediately recognized from Oliver Stone's *Platoon*.

It was Adagio for Strings. The scene where Elias is shot down with his arms stretched out in the crucifix pose. Went out like a G on a double-cross. It was coming faintly from a portable tape recorder that a staff member was listening to. He knew about the melancholy of borrowed time, but didn't know that sorrow could sound so good. He tapped on the observation window and respectfully signaled for him to turn up the volume. This request was denied, but he did turn on the cell's mic to pipe in the music.

Next he heard movement. It was Antonín Dvořák, and it was a sound that his heart would forever covet. The sound that he would later hum to himself in tens of dozens of other cells. The sound that would help him imagine new worlds. Music had always been important, since his days in juvie when the other little gangsters sang a capellas to one another. If freedom had a sound, it was the songs they sang to one another the night before each one was sent away. They sang to one another because their lives were too short and their sentences too long. They sang to one another to create moments of happiness in the saddest of places.

Later, he would learn that when Dvořák was the director of the National Conservatory of Music in New York City, he went on a tour of the US, and when he returned to New York and was asked what he thought was the original American music, he tied it back to the drums and chants of Native Americans and Negro spirituals. Colonial cousins of the colonial wound of indignity. The country's original sins committed against those who continued to weave the cosmos even when they were drylongso. The man his children affectionately called "the Moor" found himself back in Prague shortly thereafter, but Dvořák did presage rock and roll. Songs with morsels of sorrow that nourish satisfaction. They gave the world their pain to give it some joy, and ain't them bodies saints.

CARLOS MANUEL ÁLVAREZ is the author of *The Fallen*. He has been included in *Granta*'s "Best of Young Spanish-Language Novelists" issue as well as in *Bogotá39: New Voices from Latin America*, an anthology of the best Latin American writers under forty. He divides his time between Havana and Mexico City.

MJ BOND is a recent graduate of Bard College whose writings focus on the relationship between the body and language.

SOPHIE BRAXTON lives in Decatur, Georgia, where she works and writes.

MAHOGANY L. BROWNE is a writer, organizer, educator, and founder of the diverse-lit initiative Woke Baby Book Fair. She is the first-ever poet in residence at Lincoln Center in New York City, and she writes poems to fight the silence around mass incarceration, as well as YA novels in verse, live from Planet Brooklyn.

HEATHER CLEARY's translations include María Ospina's *Variations on the Body*, Betina González's *American Delirium*, and Roque Larraquy's *Comemadre* (nominee for the 2018 National Book Award). A member of the Cedilla & Co. translation collective, she has served as a judge for several national translation awards and was a founding editor of the digital, bilingual *Buenos Aires Review*. She teaches at Sarah Lawrence College.

CLAUDINA DOMINGO was born in Mexico City in 1982. As a poet, she has published the collection *Tránsito* (2011) and *Ya sabes que no veo de noche* (2017). She also published the short-story collection *Las enemigas* (2017) and the novel *La noche en el espejo* (2020). She likes to entwine Mexican History and onereic worlds.

YÁSNAYA ELENA AGUILAR GIL (from Ayutla Mixe, Oaxaca) is part of Colmix, a collective of Mixe scholars, artists, and activists dedicated to researching and disseminating Mixe history, language, and culture. She has been involved in the development of materials written in Mixe and in creating a readership in Mixe and other Indigenous languages; her work as an activist also includes language-rights defense and promoting the use of Indigenous languages in the digital sphere and in literary translation.

LIA GARCÍA (LA NOVIA SIRENA) is a pedagogue, poet, and performance artist based in Mexico City. Her trans performances take place in public spaces and are made through tenderness as a political proposal.

NIMMI GOWRINATHAN is a writer, scholar, activist, and the founder of the Politics of Sexual Violence Initiative at the City College of New York. Her recent book, *Radicalizing Her: Why Women Choose Violence* (Beacon Press, 2021), examines the complex politics of the female fighter.

GABRIELA JAUREGUI is a writer, translator, and editor. She is the author of *Many Fiestas!* (Gato Negro, 2017), *Leash Seeks Lost Bitch* (Song Cave, 2016), and *Controlled Decay* (Akashic Books, 2008), as well as the short-story collection *La memoria de las cosas* (Sexto Piso, 2015). She also edited and coauthored two essay collections: *Tsunami* and *Tsunami 2* (Sexto Piso, 2018 and 2021, respectively). She teaches English literature at the National Autonomous University of Mexico and lives and works in the forests belonging to the Mazahua people and the monarch butterflies.

LAIA JUFRESA is a Mexican author and transformational coach based in Scotland. She coaches more than seventy female writers through her online membership program, Escribir es un lugar. She is currently at work on her second novel, *Wishbone*.

JULIA WONG KCOMT was born into a tusán (Chinese Peruvian) family in Chepén, Peru, in 1965. She traveled from an early age, and her perceptions of country borders, different cultures, and diversity in ethnicity and religion became a strong motivation to write. She is the author of seventeen volumes of poetry, including *La desmineralización de los árboles* and *18 poemas de fake love para Keanu Reeves*; five books of fiction; and two collections of hybrid prose. She currently lives between Lima and Lisbon.

SABRINA HELEN LI is a writer from New Jersey. She is a student at the Iowa Writers' Workshop.

RONALDO LOPES DE OLIVEIRA is an artist with a background in philosophy, theater, and architecture. Born and raised in São Paulo, he studied at Otis College of Art and Design and El Camino College in Los Angeles, and graduated with a degree in architecture and urban planning. He began his art and architecture practice in Brazil and continued practicing in California after immigrating with his young family in the mid-'80s.

BRENDA LOZANO is a novelist, essayist, and editor. Her first novel was *Todo nada* (Tusquets Editores, 2009), followed by *Cuaderno ideal* (Alfaguara, 2014), and the short-story collection *Cómo piensan las piedras* (Alfaguara, 2017). She has been recognized as one of the most important Mexican writers under 40 by Mexico's National Council for Culture and Arts (Conaculta), the Hay Festival, and the British Council; she is also one of the Bogotá 39. Her most recent novel is *Brujas* (Alfaguara, 2020, forthcoming as *Witches* with Catapult Books and MacLehose Press). She writes regularly for the newspaper *El país* and lives in Mexico City.

VALERIA LUISELLI is the author of the award-winning novels *Faces in the Crowd* (2014), *The Story of My Teeth* (2015), and *Lost Children Archive* (2019); and the nonfiction volumes *Sidewalks* (2014) and *Tell Me How It Ends: An Essay in Forty Questions* (2017). Luiselli is the recipient of a Guggenheim and a MacArthur Fellowship. She teaches at Bard College.

MEGAN MCDOWELL is the recipient of a 2020 Award in Literature from the American Academy of Arts and Letters, among other awards, and her books have been short- and long-listed four times for the International Booker Prize. Her translations have appeared in publications including the *New Yorker*, the *Paris Review*, the *Atlantic*, and *Harper's Magazine*. She lives in Santiago, Chile.

C. T. MEXICA is a reformed gangster and former prisoner with a doctorate in comparative literature. He is a 2018 Art for Justice Bearing Witness Fellow and a 2019 PEN America Writing for Justice Fellow. He plays tiddledywinks competitively and is currently writing a memoir.

JULIA SANCHES was born in São Paulo and is the author of more than a dozen translations from Spanish, Portuguese, and Catalan into English. Her translations and writing have appeared in *Granta*, *Literary Hub*, the *Paris Review Daily*, and the *Common*, among other publications. She has received support for her work from the PEN Heim Translation Fund, PEN Translates, and the New York State Council on the Arts. Julia sits on the Authors Guild Council, where she advocates for fairer terms for literary translators.

SAMANTA SCHWEBLIN is the author of the novel *Fever Dream*, which was a finalist for the International Booker Prize. Her second novel, *Kentukis*, and the story collection *Mouthful of Birds* were long-listed for the International Booker Prize. Her books have been translated into more than thirty languages, and her work has appeared in the *New Yorker* and *Harper's Magazine*. Originally from Buenos Aires, she lives in Berlin.

JENNIFER SHYUE is a translator focusing on contemporary Cuban and Asian Peruvian writers. Her translation of *Vice-royal-ties* by Julia Wong Kcomt is forthcoming from Ugly Duckling Presse's Señal chapbook series. She can be found at shyue.co.

EDMUNDO PAZ SOLDÁN is a Bolivian writer who teaches Latin American literature at Cornell University. His books have been translated into twelve languages. His latest titles include the short-story collection *La vía del futuro* and the novel *Allá afuera hay monstruos*, both published in 2021.

JENNA TANG is a Taiwanese writer and literary translator based in New York. She translates from Chinese and Spanish. She received her MFA in fiction creative writing from the New School. Her translations and interviews have been published in *Latin American Literature Today*, *World Literature Today*, *Catapult*, and *Words without Borders*, and by Restless Books and the Asian American Writers' Workshop. She is one of the selected translators for the 2021 American Literary Translators Association Emerging Translator Mentorship Program with a focus on Taiwanese prose.

KARLA CORNEJO VILLAVICENCIO is a writer living in New Haven. *The Undocumented Americans* is her first book.

GABRIELA WIENER is a Peruvian writer and journalist living in Madrid. She has published the books *Sexographies*, *Nine Moons*, *Llamada perdida* (Missed call), *Dicen de mí* (What they say about me), and a poetry collection, *Ejercicios para el endurecimiento del espíritu* (Exercises for the hardening of the spirit). Her texts have appeared in national and international anthologies and have been translated into English, Portuguese, Polish, French, and Italian. Her first stories were published in the Peruvian narrative journalism magazine *Etiqueta Negra*. She was editor in chief of the Spanish edition of *Marie Claire* and regularly publishes opinion columns for ElDiario.es and *Vice* and the *New York Times en Español*, as well as a video column on LaMula.pe. She won her country's National Journalism Award for an investigative report on a case of gender violence. She is the creator of several performances she has staged with her family. She recently wrote and starred in the play *Qué locura enamorarme yo de ti* (How crazy to fall in love with you), directed by Mariana de

Althaus. In October of 2021, Literatura Random House will publish her novel *Huaco retrato*, which her piece in this issue is excerpted from.

KAREN TEI YAMASHITA is the author of eight books, including *I Hotel*, a finalist for the National Book Award, and, most recently, *Sansei and Sensibility*, all published by Coffee House Press. A recipient of the John Dos Passos Prize for Literature and of a US Artists Ford Foundation Fellowship, she is a currently Dickson Emeritus Professor of Literature and Creative Writing at the University of California, Santa Cruz.

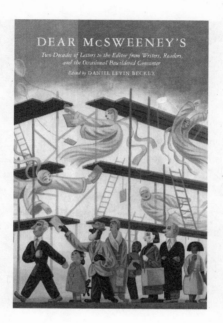

DEAR McSWEENEY'S: TWO DECADES OF LETTERS TO THE EDITOR FROM WRITERS, READERS, AND THE OCCASIONAL BEWILDERED CONSUMER

edited by Daniel Levin Becker

Since 1998, *Timothy McSweeney's Quarterly Concern* has been receiving letters to the editor: dispatches, pleas, confessions, treatises, ruminations, rants, raves, and at least one misdirected customer service query. Gathered here are one hundred installments from this sprawling one-to-many correspondence, including but not limited to musings on moths and mummies, macaroons and cats, armadillos and homicidal sea worms, and the arcana of Jerry Lewis's acting career—all from some of the brightest contemporary voices in... well, American letters.

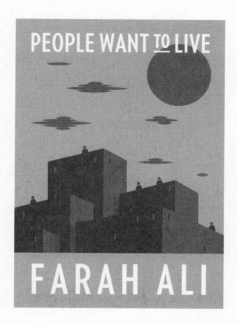

"*Farah Ali writes with a precise and profound understanding of the most vital dimensions of the human experiencd... a thrilling and essential new voice.*"
—Laura van den Berg, author of *I Hold a Wolf by the Ears*

PEOPLE WANT TO LIVE
by Farah Ali

Set in Pakistan, the award-winning stories in *People Want to Live* follow people on the brink of abandonment—in their personal relationships and their place in the world. Farah Ali's debut collection of fourteen stories features tales of togetherness and reckless faith in the face of a world that's built to break us. Her characters battle loneliness and, in their fight, reveal surprising vulnerabilities and an astonishing measure of hope.

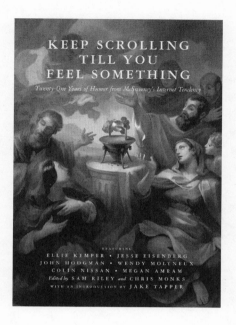

ALSO AVAILABLE
FROM McSWEENEY'S

FICTION

POETRY

COLLINS LIBRARY

ALL THIS AND MORE AT

STORE.MCSWEENEYS.NET

Founded in 1998, McSweeney's is an independent publisher based in San Francisco. McSweeney's exists to champion ambitious and inspired new writing, and to challenge conventional expectations about where it's found, how it looks, and who participates. We're here to discover things we love, help them find their most resplendent form, and place them into the hands of curious, engaged readers.

THERE ARE SEVERAL WAYS TO SUPPORT MCSWEENEY'S:

Support Us on Patreon
visit *www.patreon.com/mcsweeneysinternettendency*

Subscribe & Shop
visit *store.mcsweeneys.net*

Volunteer & Intern
email *eric@mcsweeneys.net*

Sponsor Books & *Quarterlies*
email *amanda@mcsweeneys.net*

To learn more, please visit *www.mcsweeneys.net/donate* or contact Executive Director Amanda Uhle at *amanda@mcsweeneys.net* or 415.642.5609.

McSweeney's Literary Arts Fund is a nonprofit organization as described by IRS 501(c)(3). Your support is invaluable to us.